Ancora una volta dedichiamo questo libro ai nostri cari
mamme, papà, nonne fratelli e sorelle
che ci hanno supportato e "sopportato" sempre

From my Florentine Kitchen

From my Florentine Kitchen™
More than 60 recipes in 10 easy menus

White Lily LLC
332 Bleecker St. F4#
10014 NY, New York
www.whitelilyusa.com
customer@whitelilyusa.com

Ordering Information:
Quantity sales. Special discounts are available on quantity purchases by corporations, associations, and others. For details, contact the authors at the address above.

First Edition
2013

Authors:
Varinia Cappelletti: *Recipe development, Editorial director, Design director, Food stylist*
Edoardo Cecotto: *Photograph, Design Director, Cover Design, Cover art and illustrations*

We have decided to write this book after eight years, during which we have been devoted, we hope successfully, to gratifying the palate of our guests!

The book appeals to all those who love good food, but it is also for those who do not know how to cook!
As a result it will not be a collection of recipes, but the presentation of a method.

This method encompasses learning how to make the right ingredient purchases, respecting the timetables, knowing the flavors, encouraging imagination and finally becoming little chefs!

Ten menus: easy, savory and smart.

We hope you enjoy them, and buon appetito!

INDEX

WHY IS THIS MORE THAN A COOKBOOK?

This is not only a book. It goes beyond! Through it you'll have access to **extra contents.**

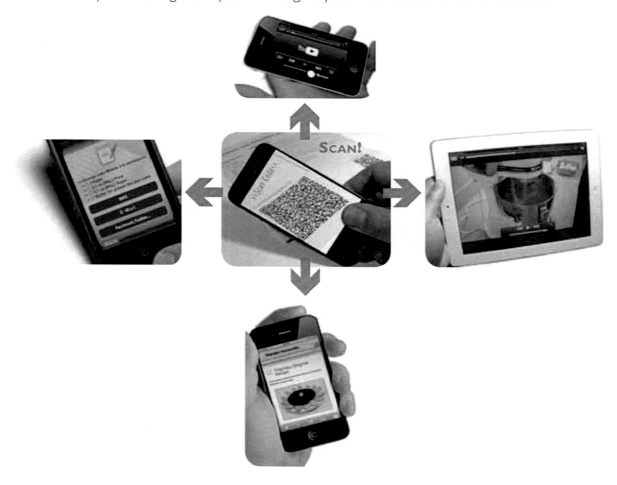

With this code, you'll have the ability to access more information from any smartphone, tablet or computer. There is software free for **iPhone, iPad,** and all devices with **Android, Windows Mobile, Nokia OS,** etc.

HOW DO I USE THE QR CODE?
Start the program on your device, point the camera at the QR Code.
What information does it contain?
- Ingredient list with quantities
- Extra content like recipe variations, tips, photos and video

QR CODE TIPS
If your device can not read QR Code:
- *The code is not sufficiently well lit*
- *You have not held your device still enough to read the code*
- *Dirt or other substances on the lens can cause an incorrect reading*
- *The surface on which the code is printed is dirty or damaged*
- *Your device can not read QR Codes*

List of QR code compatible sotware: http://florentinekitchen.com

Menù N 1 Leonardo

ANTIPASTO
Mozzarella mousse with cucumber

PRIMO
Dumplings with pinach and Ricotta

SECONDO
Chicken cacciatora

DOLCE
Panna cotta

MOUSSE DI MOZZARELLA CON CETRIOLO

Mozzarella mousse with cucumber

TOTAL TIME: 25
PREP: 15
COOK: 5
LEVEL: easy

INGREDIENTS

MAKES 4 SERVINGS

* 3½FL OZ (100 ML) HEAVY CREAM
* 2 PACKETS OF GELATINE
* 9 OZ (250 G) MOZZARELLA (BUFFALO MOZZARELLA WOULD BE BETTER)
* SALT AND FRESHLY GROUND BLACK PEPPER
* EXTRA-VIRGIN OLIVE OIL, FOR DRIZZLING
* 1 CUCUMBER CUT IN VERY THIN SLICES

READ SHOPPING LIST

DIRECTIONS

1. **Warm** the cream in a pan
2. **Dissolve** the gelatine in the cream and stir thoroughly
3. **Pour** over the mozzarella and blend with a hand blender to a smooth paste. Set in the fridge
4. **Add** a drizzle of Extra-virgin olive oil
5. **Lay** two spoonfuls of mozzarella mousse on the dish and hem in with the slices of cucumber

GNUDI SPINACI E RICOTTA

Dumplings with pinach and Ricotta cheese

TOTAL TIME: 40
PREP: 20
COOK: 20
LEVEL: easy

INGREDIENTS

MAKES 4 SERVINGS

- 1/2 LB. (250 G.) RICOTTA CHEESE
- 1/2 LB. (250 G.) STEAMED SPINACH
- 2 TBSP EXTRA- VIRGIN OLIVE OIL
- 1/4 LB. (125 G.) GRATED PARMIGIANO
- 1 EGG
- PINCH OF FRESHLY GRATED NUTMEG
- SALT AND PEPPER
- 3 TBSP OF ALL-PURPOSE FLOUR, PLUS 1 CUP FOR COATING
- POPPY SEADS

READ SHOPPING LIST

DIRECTIONS

1. **Sauté** (medium fire for 5-7 minutes) with 2 Tbsp Extra-virgin olive oil the steamed spinach with a bit of salt and pepper
2. **Wait** until it has gone cold
3. **Chop** the spinach
4. **In a large bowl**, mix ricotta, spinach, Parmigiano, egg, nutmeg and flour
5. **Form** mixture into small balls
6. **Lay the Gnudi** on a tray covered with baking paper coated with flour
7. **Cover** and put in the refrigerator until ready to cook (or minimum for one hour)
8. **Bring** a large pot of salted water to a boil
9. **Dredge** the formed gnudi in flour to coat, tapping off the excess
10. **Slide** formed Gnudi into the boiling water. Be careful
11. **Remove** the Gnudi using a slotted spoon after they float to the top and have cooked for about 2 or 3 minutes.
12. **Arrange** gnudi on a platter and lightly drizzle with butter, truffle and Parmigiano

From My Florentine Kitchen

POLLO ALLA CACCIATORA
Chicken cacciatora

TOTAL TIME: 45
PREP: 15
COOK: 40
LEVEL: easy

INGREDIENTS

MAKES 4 SERVINGS

- **8 CHICKEN** THIGHS- BONELESS AND SKINLESS
- **1/2 CUP** STARCH FLOUR OR RICE FLOUR (GLUTEN FREE)
- **1/2 GLASS** EXTRA-VIRGIN OLIVE OIL
- **1 ONION** CHOPPED (WHITE OR YELLOW)
- **2 CARROTS** CHOPPED
- **3 CELERY** STICKS CHOPPED
- **1 GARLIC** CLOVE, FINELY CHOPPED
- **1** GLASS OF RED WINE
- **1 (28 OZ)** CAN OF DICED TOMATOES
- **3 TBSP** PASTE TOMATOES
- **2 ROSEMARY** SPRIGS
- **HOT WATER**
- **SALT AND PEPPER**

READ SHOPPING LIST

DIRECTIONS

1. **Sprinkle** the chicken pieces with flour to coat lightly
2. **In a large** heavy sauce pan, heat the oil over a medium-high flame
3. **Add** the chicken pieces to the pan and saute just until brown, about 5 minutes per side.
4. **Add** the onion, garlic, celery and carrots
5. **Season** with salt and pepper
6. **Add** the tomato paste
7. **Add** the wine and simmer
8. **Add** the tomatoes and rosemary
9. **Continue** simmering, covered, over medium-low heat until the chicken is just cooked through, about 25-30 minutes
10. **If** it becomes dry add the warm water

PANNA COTTA

Panna cotta

TOTAL TIME: 20
PREP: 10
COOK: 10
LEVEL: easy

INGREDIENTS

MAKES **4** SERVINGS

- 17 FL OZ. (1/2 L) OF CREAM
- 3 TSBP OF SUGAR
- 1/2 CUP (1 DL) OF MILK
- 0,35 OZ (10 G) OF GELATINE POWDER

READ SHOPPING LIST

DIRECTIONS

1. Pour the ingredients into a saucepan
2. Mix well with a whisk
3. Heat on very low heat and bring to a boil
4. Boil for two minutes, stirring
5. Fill the cups
6. Place in the refrigerator (one hour minimum) to harden

From My Florentine Kitchen

SUGGESTIONS

FAST AND EASY MOZZARELLA MOUSSE! NO COOKED

INGREDIENTS
- OZ. 8,8 (250G) MOZZARELLA (BUFFALO WOULD BE BETTER)
- 1 CUP WHOLE MILK
- 1 CUP FRESH CREAM
- 3 TBSP EXTRAVIRGIN OLIVE OIL
- PINCH OF SALT
- RED CHILLY
- LEAVES OF BASIL

DIRECTIONS
1. Mix all ingredient and blend until the consistence is soft, creamy but hold up.
2. Serve with basil and cucumber (follow the indication pag)

CON GLI GNUDI PUOI FARE ANDHE LE CREPS ALLA FIORENTINA ...
WITH DUMPLINGS RICOTTA AND SPINACH... YOU CAN DO ALSO THE CREPS IN FLORENTINE STYLE!

INGREDIENTS
YOU NEED A NONSTICK PAN (ABOUT 8" - 10" DIAMETER).
- 1 CUP FLOUR
- 1/8 TEASPOON SALT
- 4 EGGS PER PERSON
- 1 CUP MILK
- 2 TBSP BUTTER, MELTED

DIRECTIONS
1. Whisk everything in a bowl until smooth
2. Heat up a nonstick pan over medium-high heat.
3. Using a ladle, pour a few tablespoons of batter onto the center of the pan.
4. Swirl the pan around so batter evenly coats the sides.
5. Return the pan to heat.
6. The batter will quickly dry
7. To turn the crepe over.
8. Use the spatula to flip over the crepe. (no metal)
9. It's perfectly acceptable to use your fingers if necessary
10. Finish cooking the crepe (about 30 seconds for the second side to cook)
11. Gently slide it out onto a plate.
12. You can stack the crepes
13. To fill the crepe.
14. Place the filling in on one the crepe (about 0,19" thikness)
15. Using your fingers, roll the crepe around the filling
16. You can also fold the crep in half and again half (you'll obtain a triangle)

CREPS ARE GOOD ALSO STUFFED WITH SIMPLE RICOTTA AND PARMIGIANO TOSSED WITH MEAT SAUCE!

Menu' N 2 Giotto

ANTIPASTO
Bread salad (cold) with tomatoes, onion, basil and cucumber

PRIMO
Pasta with Pesto with pistachios and tomatoes confit

SECONDO
Chicken Fricassea (with lemon and egg)

DOLCE
"Rich" Cream Chantilly...

PANZANELLA

Bread salad (cold) with tomatoes, onion, basil and cucumber

TOTAL TIME: 25
PREP: 25
COOK: 0
LEVEL: easy

INGREDIENTS

MAKES 4 SERVINGS

- WHITE WINE VINEGAR
- 15 LEAVES BASIL (OR MORE
- 1 CUCUMBER
- 1 RED ONION (TROPEA QUALITY)
- EXTRA-VIRGIN OLIVE OIL
- 4 THICK SLICES OF RUSTIC BREAD LOAF (STALE) (TUSCAN)
- GROUND BLACK PEPPER
- 2 RIPE SALAD TOMATOES
- CAPERS (IF YOU LIKE BUT ARE NOT IN THE ORIGINAL RECIPE)
- SALT

DIRECTIONS

1. **Cut** the onion into thin slices and put them to soak in a bowl.
2. **Cover** it with water and a 1 or 2 tablespoons of vinegar for at least two hours.
3. **Peel** the cucumber and cut the cucumber into thin slices
4. **Cut** the tomatoes into small cubes
5. **Cut** 4 slices of bread, remove the crust and dip them into cold water and vinegar until they become soft
6. **Squeeze** the bread slices and chop them
7. **In** a bowl add the red onion (drained of its water)
8. **Add** the tomatoes, seeded cucumber and basil leaves by hand
9. **Mix** gently
10. **Season** with salt, pepper and a little extra-virgin olive oil
11. **If** you like you can add vinegar
12. **Then** lay the panzanella
in the refrigerator for at least an hour

READ SHOPPING LIST

Pasta al pesto di pisatcchi e pomodori confit

Pasta with Pesto with pistachios and tomatoes confit

TOTAL TIME: 2 h.
PREP: 20
COOK: 1.30 h
LEVEL: easy

INGREDIENTS

MAKES 4 SERVINGS

FRESH PASTA 60 GR. PER PERSON
(HALF OZ. FOR 4)
FOR PESTO WITH PISTACHIOS*
SEE THE RECIPES

INGREDIENTS FOR TOMATOES CONFIT
* 16 CHERRY TOMATOES
* 4 SPRIGS OF THYME
* 1 CLOVE OF GARLIC FINELY SLICED
* 2 TBSP OF SUGAR
* SALT AND PEPPER
* EXTRA-VIRGIN OLIVE OIL

DIRECTIONS

1. **Center** a rack in the oven and preheat the oven to 200 degrees F. Line a baking sheet with foil and pour about 2 tablespoons of olive oil evenly over the pan
2. **Cut** each tomato lengthwise in half carefully
3. **Lay** the tomato halves in the pan
4. **Give** the tops of the tomatoes a light coat of olive oil
5. **Season** the tops of the tomatoes with salt and pepper and a little sugar, and scatter over the garlic and thyme.
6. **Slide** the pan into the oven and bake the tomatoes for 1 hour and a half, or until they are very tender but still able to hold their shape
7. **Cook** pasta in a large pot of boiling salted water until done.
8. **Drain** in a large bowl, mix pesto, stir in Parmigiano cheese
9. **Serve,** adding the Tomatoes confit to the dish

READ SHOPPING LIST

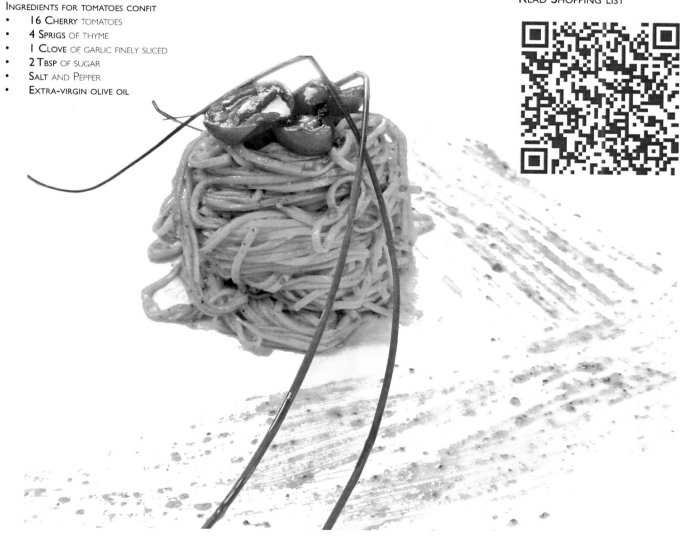

POLLO IN FRICASSEA

Chicken Fricassea (with lemon and egg)

TOTAL TIME: 25
PREP: 15
COOK: 25
LEVEL: easy

INGREDIENTS

MAKES 4 SERVINGS

- HALF CHICKEN BREAST CUT INTO CUBES (1 INCH)
- 1/4 CUP ALL-PURPOSE FLOUR OR STARCH OR RICE FLOUR (GLUTEN FREE)
- 2 TBSP BUTTER
- 1 CUP CHICKEN BROTH
- 1 LEMON JUICE (2 IF YOU LIKE)
- 2 YOLKS
- SALT AND PEPPER

READ SHOPPING LIST

DIRECTIONS

1. **Coat** the chicken lightly in flour
2. **Heat** in a large skillet the butter, and add the cubes of chicken breast. Cook until they are brown (6 or 8 minutes)
3. **Add** salt and pepper
4. **Add** stock. When it has evaporated, remove the pan from heat
5. **Add** the lemon juice and yolks
6. **Stir** and serve

CREMA CHANTILLY ....ARRICCHITA

"Rich" Cream Chantilly....

TOTAL TIME: 10
PREP: 10
COOK: 0
LEVEL: easy

INGREDIENTS

MAKES 4 SERVINGS

- 2 CUPS HEAVY CREAM
- 3 TBSP ICING SUGAR
- 1 TSP VANILLA EXTRACT
- 3 YOLKS

READ SHOPPING LIST

DIRECTIONS

1. **In** a large mixing bowl, beat the heavy cream, and vanilla extract together on high speed until soft peaks form in the mixture
2. **In** a different large mixing bowl, beat the yolks with icing sugar high speed until soft peaks form in the mixture
3. **Gently** combine the whipped cream to the yolks mixture
4. **Place** in refrigerator (minimum one hour)

SUGGESTIONS

PANZANELLA
Bread salad (cold) with tomatoes, onion, basil and cucumber

THE TUSCAN BREAD

This traditional Tuscan bread is as simple as bread can be: it's just yeast, water and flour mixed together, kneaded, shaped and baked. Salt is the missing element here.

The reason is unclear; some sources say that centuries ago, the government levied a hefty tax on salt that the Tuscans didn't want to pay. Whatever the reason, the strong flavors of Tuscan cuisine are well-suited to a less strongly-flavored bread.

The tuscan bread is made with a flour no too rich of gluten and the absence of salt don't preserves the gluten.

So the the bread is not "elastic", and the crumb is dense.

If you use other quality of bread, rich of gluten, don't melts with the liquids (water, vinagre, tomatoes etc...) amalgamating all ingredients but, becomes gummy and not well mixed with all ingredients.

MY PERSONAL VARIANT OF PANZANELLA

PANZANELLA WITH HAM
Lay two spoonfuls of Panzanella on the dish and hem in with the slices of ham

PANZANELLA WITH TUNA FISH
I can of Tuna finsh (natural or with Extravirgin Olive Oil)
Mince the Tuna fish very well
Mix with all ingredients

LAMB IN FRICASSEA

INGREDIENTS
- 2 LB. LEAN LAMB SHOULDER OR LEG, CUT IN SMALL STEWING PIECES
- SALT AND FRESHLY GROUND BLACK PEPPER TO TASTE
- 2 CLOVES GARLIC
- 5-6 TBSP EXTRA VIRGIN OLIVE OIL
- I SPRIG ROSEMARY, LEAVES ONLY, CHOPPED
- I CUP DRY WHITE WINE
- 2 EGGS
- FRESHLY SQUEEZED JUICE OF I LEMON

DIRECTIONS
1. **In** a heavy saucepan or casserole add Oil, rosemary and the pieces of lamb and continue cooking over medium-low, turning the lamb frequently until all of the pieces have lost their rosy color
2. **Stir** in the wine and raise the heat to medium.
3. **Add** the broth and stir once more
4. **Cover** the pan, lower the heat again, and barely simmer the lamb about I hour, checking from time to time and adding a little more broth if it seems necessary
5. **When** the lamb is done, beat the eggs very well with the lemon juice.
6. **Add** the sauce to the stew to the egg-lemon mixture, beating well
7. **The** heat of the lamb should be sufficient to thicken the eggs slightly to make a velvety sauce that envelops the pieces of lamb
8. **If** it's still too liquid, return the pan to very low heat, or set in a pan of simmering water, and cook, stirring without cease until the sauce has reached the desired consistency

Menu' N 3 Botticelli

ANTIPASTO
Raw vegetables may be diped
with garlic sauce

PRIMO
Carrot soup

SECONDO
Lam chops with artchockes

DOLCE
Tiramisù with strawberry

PINZIMONIO CON "AGLIATA"

Raw vegetables may be dipped with garlic sauce

TOTAL TIME: 40
PREP: 20
COOK: 30
LEVEL: easy

INGREDIENTS

MAKES 4 SERVINGS

- 1 OR 2 WHOLE HEADS OF GARLIC
- 1,5 OZ (40 G.) STALE BREADCRUMBS (TUSCAN BREAD OR SIMILAR. NO BAGUETTE OR "CIABATTA" OR "FOCACCIA")
- 2 CUPS OF CHICKEN STOCK
- PINCH OF GINGER
- PINCH OF NUTMEG
- SALT AND PEPPER

ROW VEGETABLES
- CUCUMBERS
- CARROTS
- RED AND YELLOW BELL PEPPERS
- RADISH
- FRESH ONIONS
- SWEET ARTICHOKES
- TOMATOES
- 4-5 TBSP PER PERSON EXTRA VIRGIN OLIVE OIL
- FRESH POUNDED BLACK PEPPER
- SALT

READ SHOPPING LIST

DIRECTIONS

PER AGLIATA SAUCE
1. **Preheat** oven to 350-400 degrees F (175 degrees C)
2. **Cut** aluminum foil large enough to wrap each garlic head
3. **Place** 1 teaspoon of Extra-virgin olive oil in each square of foil and place one garlic head into each square of foil
4. **Fold** the packets up, and arrange them in a pie pan
5. **Bake** for 30 minutes, or until the garlic is soft
6. **Allow** the garlic to cool
7. **Use** a fork or your fingers to pull or squeeze the roasted garlic cloves out of their skins
8. **Dip** the breadcrumbs in the chicken broth
9. **Mix** with the squeezed garlic and all the other ingredients
10. **Add** the rest of the chicken stock
11. **Cook** until it begins to boil (for 2 or 3 minutes)
12. **Serve** warm

HOW TO PREPARE YOU ROW VEGETABLE

1. **Cut** the vegetables into long strips
2. **Place** your sliced veggies on a plate of flat bowl
3. **Pour** oil into a small bowl and add all other spices and additions
4. **Dip** sliced veggies into the spiced oil and relish

ZUPPA DI CAROTE

Carrot soup

TOTAL TIME: 40
PREP: 10
COOK: 40
LEVEL: easy

INGREDIENTS

MAKES **4** SERVINGS

- **4 T**BSP EXTRA-VIRGIN OLIVE OIL
- **2 T**BSP BUTTER
- **1 M**EDIUM ONION, CHOPPED
- **2 M**EDIUM CARROTS PER PERSON
- **2 C**ELERY STICKS, MEDIUM -SMALL STICKS
- **2 P**INCHES FRESH THYME MINCED
- **6 C**UPS VEGETABLE STOCK
- **6 B**LADES FRESH CHIVES, CUT INTO 1-INCH PIECES

READ SHOPPING LIST

DIRECTIONS

1. **Peel** and slice the carrots
2. **Steam** the carrots for 15-20 minutes (microwawe or steamer basket)
3. **Chop** the onion and celery
4. **In** a pot melt the butter with oil
5. **Add** the carrots, onion and celery, salt, pepper and thyme
6. **Cook** untill the onion and celery are well done (no burn...)
7. **With** hand mixer reduce the ingredients to a puree
8. **Add** the vegetable stock until the puree has the right consistency of cream (don't stop to use the hand mixer when you add the stock)

From My Florentine Kitchen

COSTOLETTE DI AGNELLO CON CARCIOFI

Lam chops with artchockes

TOTAL TIME: 40
PREP: 20
COOK: 40
LEVEL: easy

INGREDIENTS

MAKES 4 SERVINGS

- 8 LAMB CUTLETS
- 4 ARTICHOKES
- 1 LEMON JUICE
- 1/2 CUP OF DRY WHITE WINE
- 2 TBSP OF BUTTER
- 1/2 CUP OF EXTRA VIRGIN OLIVE OIL
- 2 TBSP CHOPPED PARSLEY
- 1 CLOVE OF GARLIC
- SALT AND PEPPER

DIRECTIONS

1. **Cut** the artichokes then slice them into 8 wedges
2. **Put** the artichokes, clean, in a basin of water acidulated to prevent the formation of black parts which, remember, must be eliminated
3. **In** a frying pan with a little oil, fry gently 1 clove of garlic
4. **Then** add the sliced artichokes
5. **Add** salt, cover with a lid, lower the heat and cook (it will take 10 minutes), add the chopped parsley at the end
6. **In** a saucepan, melt the butter in a drizzle of extra virgin olive oil
7. **Fry** over high heat
8. **Pour** the white wine
9. **Let** it evaporate for 3/4 a torch high
10. **Add** the artichokes
11. **Cook** for 7/8 minutes

READ SHOPPING LIST

Tiramisù con Ricotta alle Fragole
Ricotta Tiramisù with strawberry

Total Time: 25
Prep: 15
Cook: 5
Level: easy

INGREDIENTS

Makes 4 servings

- 1/2 Cup (113 g.) Mascarpone cheese (room temperature)
- 1/2 Cup (113 g.) Ricotta cheese
- 3 Yolks
- 4 Tbsp of sugar
- 10 Strawberries cut into
- 3 Tbsp of sugar for make a syrup
- 1 Cup of Limoncello
- Ladyfingers Quantity: For Glasses and Bowls: 2-4 for glass (1-2 for layers)

DIRECTIONS

For Compote
1. **Cut** the strawberry
2. **Add** the 3 Tbsp of sugar
3. **Put** on the low heat and cook until the syrup become dense (30 minutes)

For Tiramisu
1. **In** a bowl, beat the egg yolks, adding 3 Tbsp of sugar
2. **Beat** until the mixture has a consistency of mousse (about 3-4 minutes)
3. **Add** the mascarpone and ricotta cheeses to the egg yolk mixture
4. **Beat** quickly at a reduced speed until creamy
5. **Dip** each Ladyfinger into the Limoncello for only 2-3 seconds
6. **Place** a layer of the "Basic cream" and then the Ladyfingers soaked in a Limoncello.
7. **Repeat** for 2 layers.
8. **On** top add the strawberries compote

From My Florentine Kitchen

SUGGESTIONS

HOW TO TRIM ARTICHOKES

- CUT OFF AND DISCARD STEM END
- PULL OFF AND DISCARD TOUGH OUTER LEAVES, STARTING WITH THE OUTER RING AND WORKING YOUR WAY AROUND AND IN (KEEP GOING-- PULLING OFF AND DISCARDING LEAVES--AS LEAVES TURN TENDER AND YELLOW)
- CUT OFF AND DISCARD CROWN OF ARTICHOKE
- USE SCISSORS TO CUT OFF AND DISCARD THORNY TOPS
- GRAB THE TOP OF THE CENTER, PURPLE-TIPPED LEAVES AND PULL TO REMOVE THEM
- USE A PARING KNIFE TO CUT OFF AND DISCARD ANY TOUGH, FIBROUS, DARK GREEN PARTS CLINGING TO THE OUTSIDE OF THE HEART
- PUT THE ARTICHOKES, CLEAN, IN A BASIN OF WATER ACIDULATED TO PREVENT THE FORMATION OF BLACK PARTS WHICH, REMEMBER, MUST BE ELIMINATED.

ARTICHOKES IN ROMAN STYLE WITH ROAST CHICKEN

INGREDIENTS
MAKE 4 SERVING
- 8 ARTICHOKES (PREFERABLY ROMANS) CLEAN
- 1 CLOVE OF GARLIC
- 2 TBSP CHOPPED MINT (FRESH IF POSSIBLE)
- 1 GLASS EXTRA VIRGIN OLIVE OIL
- 2 TBSP CHOPPED PARSLEY (FRESH IF POSSIBLE)
- SALT

FOR CHICKEN
- 4 BONELESS LEG
- 1 TBSP MINCHED THYME
- 1 TBSP MINCED ROSEMARY
- 3 TBSP EXTRA VIRGIN OLIVE OIL
- 2 TBSP CHOPPED PARSLEY (FRESH IF PO

1. Roast the Chicken legs with thyme and rosemary
2. Add 3 Tbsp of Extra Virgin Olive Oil in a non-stick pan
3. Add the thyme and rosemary chopped
4. Cook the Chicken legs in a both side until are golden
5. Add a cup of white wine and salt
6. Cook for 10 minutes cover with lid
7. Cook for 5 minutes without lid
8. Minche 2 artichokes and add it to the chicken
9. Serve with artichikes

1. Chop the garlic, mint and parsley and add a little olive oil and a pinch of salt
2. Fill the artichokes with the filling
3. Put the artichokes on a salted surface
4. Add plenty of oil
5. Bake (<u>covered</u>) for 7 minutes
6. Turn off the heat for 5 minutes
7. Cook again for 5 minutes (<u>covered</u>)

VARIANT FOR CARROTS SOUP

INGREDIENTS
- CARROTS SOUP WITH BAKE LEEK WITH PARMIGIANO
- 2 TBSP BUTTER MELT
- 8 MEDIUM-LARGE LEAVES LEEKS
- 2 TSP. LIGHTLY CHOPPED FRESH THYME
- 1/3 CUP FINELY GRATED PARMIGIANO-REGGIANO

DIRECTIONS
1. **Heat** the oven to 350°F.
2. **Cut** each leek in half lengthwise
3. **Cut** the leaves in small strips
4. **Pour** the butter melt evenly over the leeks (help you with silicon brush)
5. **Sprinkle** with Parmigiano and the thyme over the leeks
6. **Bake** just until the cheese melts (golden brown)
7. **Transfer** the leeks to a cup of soup

Menù N 4 Michelangelo

ANTIPASTO PRIMO
Parmigiano Pie with Balsamic Pasta with "White" meat sauce

SECONDO DOLCE
Eggplants Parmigiana Twin Tiramisù

Sformato di Parmigiano e Aceto Balsamico

Parmigiano Pie with Balsamic

Total Time: 45
Prep: 15
Cook: 35
Level: easy

INGREDIENTS

Makes 4 servings

- 7 Oz. (200 g.) finely grated Parmigiano
- 7 Oz. (200 g.) Ricotta cheese
- Pinch of cayenne pepper
- Pinch nutmeg
- 2 Extra-large eggs
- Butter for greasing the moulds

DIRECTIONS

1. **Preheat** the oven to 400 degrees F
2. **Butter** the inside of an 8-cup souffle dish (2 1/4 inches in diameter) and sprinkle evenly with flour
3. **In** a bowl mix the Parmigiano with the eggs
4. **Add** the ricotta, pepper and nutmeg
5. **Pour** into the souffle dish and place in the middle of the oven. Turn the temperature down to 375 degrees F.
6. **Bake** for 30 to 35 minutes (don't peek!) until puffed and brown
7. **Serve** immediately
8. **Parmigiano** soufle with Balsamic

Read Shopping list

From My Florentine Kitchen

PASTA CON RAGU' BIANCO

Pasta with "White" meat sauce

TOTAL TIME: 1,45 h
PREP: 30
COOK: 1,30 h
LEVEL: easy

INGREDIENTS

MAKES 4 SERVINGS

- 1 CARROT
- 1 ONION
- 2 STALKS OF CELERY
- 2 CLOVES OF GARLIC
- 2 BAY LEAVES
- 1 SPRIG OF ROSEMARY
- 1 TBSP CHOPPED FRESH THYME
- 2-3 LEAVES SALVIA
- 1/2 LB. (250 G) MINCED BEEF MEAT
- 3,5 OZ. (100 G) PANCETTA*
- 1/4 LB. (150 G) SAUSAGE (BREAKFAST SAUSAGE NOT ITALIAN)
- 1/2 CUP EXTRA VIRGIN OLIVE OIL
- 2,5 CUPS (600 ML) DEFATTED BEEF BROTH APPROXIMATELY
- 1/2 CUP WHITE WINE
- SALT AND PEPPER

* NO BACON

READ SHOPPING LIST

DIRECTIONS

1. **Put** carrot, celery, onion, garlic, rosemary, thyme and sage in a food processor; pulse until finely chopped
2. **Over** a medium flame, heat the olive oil in a large pan
3. **Add** the chopped vegetables, herbs and 2 bay leaves
4. **Cook** until it is well done
5. **Add** the Pancetta and cook for 3-4 minutes (until the Pancetta is cooked)
6. **Add** the meat (beef or chicken) and the fresh salsiccia
7. **Add** the wine and simmer until the alcohol evaporates, about 3-5 minutes
8. **Stir** in the tomato paste and cook for 2-4 minutes
9. **Add** the broth
10. **When** the sauce starts to boil, reduce the heat so that it cooks at the barest simmer
11. **Cook**, uncovered, for 1 hour, turning down the heat if the sauce starts to scorch. If the sauce dries out before it is done, add a ladle of the broth
12. **When** it is ready add salt and pepper

From My Florentine Kitchen

PARMIGIANA DI MELANZANE

Eggplants Parmigiana

TOTAL TIME:	1,25 h
PREP:	1 h
COOK:	45
LEVEL:	easy

INGREDIENTS

MAKES 4 SERVINGS

- 2 LB. (ABOUT 2 MEDIUM-SIZED) OF EGGPLANT
- EXTRA-VIRGIN OLIVE OIL
- 3,5 OZ. (100 G.) FRESHLY GRATED PARMIGIANO REGGIANO
- 2 CUPS BASIC TOMATO SAUCE, RECIPE FOLLOWS
- 1 POUND (450 G) BALL FRESH MOZZARELLA, THINLY SLICED
- BASIL
- SALT

READ SHOPPING LIST

DIRECTIONS

1. **Preheat** the oven to 350 degrees F.
2. **Slice** the eggplant horizontally about 1/4-inch thick
3. **Place** the slices in a large colander, sprinkle with salt and set aside to rest about 15-20 minutes.
4. **Drain** and dry on towels
5. **Grill** the eggplants
6. **With** nonstick paper cover the single soufleè dishes (or similar)
7. **Alternate** a slice of grilled eggplant with Parmigiano and top each with the next smallest piece of eggplant, then sauce, then mozzarella
8. **Repeat** the layering process until all the ingredients have been used, finishing again with the Parmigiano
9. **Place** in the oven and bake until the top of each little stack is golden brown and bubbly, about 15-20 minutes

BIS DI TIRAMISU'

Twin Tiramisù

TOTAL TIME: 25
PREP: 15
COOK: 5
LEVEL: easy

INGREDIENTS

MAKES 4 SERVINGS

FOR A COFFEE TIRAMISU'
- 8 Oz. (226 G.) MASCARPONE CHEESE ROOM TEMPERATURE)
- 4 YOLKS
- 8 Oz. (226 G.) OF SUGAR
- 8 LADYFINGERS
- 1/2 CUP BLACK COFFEE (ESPRESSO)
- COCOA POWDER

FOR TIRAMISU WITH PEACH
- 1 BIG PEACH
- 4 TBSP OF SYRUP (PEACH OR CARAMEL)
- 1/2 CUP OF AMARETTO LIQUOR

READ SHOPPING LIST

DIRECTIONS

FOR A COFFEE TIRAMISU'
1. **Make** the coffee (espresso coffee); let cool in a bowl
2. **Whip** the yolks with sugar until stiff; fold the mascarpone cheese into yolk mixture thus obtaining a soft cream
3. **Pour** a spoon of mascarpone cream
4. **Arrange** one Ladyfinger (soaked ina coffee) for a single small cup
5. **Cover** with 1 or 2 spoons of mascarpone cream
6. **Add** on top the cocoa powder

FOR A TIRAMISU' WITH PEACH
1. **Cut** the peach in a small pieces
2. **Pour** a spoon of mascarpone cream
3. **Arrange** one Ladyfinger (soaked in a liquor)
4. **Add** some pieces of peach
5. **Cover** with 1 or 2 spoons of mascarpone cream
6. **Add** a spoon of syrup in top

From My Florentine Kitchen

SUGGESTIONS

Parmgiano Pie Variant (Substitute the ricotta cheese with besciamella sauce)

INGREDIENTS FOR A BESCIAMELLA SUCE
- **5 Tbsp** butter
- **4 Tbsp** flour
- **3 Cups** milk
- **2 Tsp** salt
- **1/2 Tsp** grated nutmeg (freshly)

DIRECTIONS FOR A BASCIAMELLA SUCE
1. **In** a medium saucepan, heat butter and salt until melted
2. **Add** flour and stir until smooth
3. **Over** medium heat, cook until light golden
4. **Meanwhile,** heat milk in separate pan until just about to boil
5. **Add** milk to butter mixture gradually, whisking continuously until very smooth and bring to a boil
6. **Cook** 1-2 minutes and remove from heat
7. **Season** with nutmeg

Variant for "White meat sauce". Chicken in place of beef

For prepare your chickens ragu you can use the same ingredients of the original recipe "White meat" just sostituite the chicken breast mince in place of beef.
The time of cook is shortly. No more than 1 hour!

The traditional Eggplant Parmigiana want the fry the eggplant

In place of grilled eggplant you can use the fry eggplant like the tradition wants!
Slice the eggplant horizontally about 1/4-inch thick
Place the slices in a large colander, sprinkle with salt and set aside to rest about 15-20 minutes.
Drain and dry on towels very well
Dust with flour (conflicting with some recipes that don't include the flour and other that add flour and crumb bread!)
Abundant peanuts oil (or any kind of oil for fry)
Fry the slices of eggplant and follow the same recipe

Menù N 5 Lorenzo

ANTIPASTO
Caprese with grilled zucchini

SECONDO
Savory tart with artichokes served
with onion and Balsamic

PRIMO
Bread tomatoes soup

DOLCE
Gelato with
Mascarpone and Amaretto cookies

CAPRESE CON ZUCCHINE GRIGLIATE

Caprese with grilled zucchini

TOTAL TIME: 25
PREP: 15
COOK: 10
LEVEL: easy

INGREDIENTS

MAKES 4 SERVINGS

- 1 MEDIUM ZUCCHINI, SLICED 1/4 INCH THICK
- 2 TOMATOES CUT INTO CUBES
- 5-6 BASIL LEAVES CHOPPED
- BLADES OF CHIVES FOR BUNDLING UP THE TOMATOES WITH THE ZUCCHINI
- 4-5 TBSP EXTRA VIRGIN OLIVE OIL
- SALT AND PEPPER
- 1 CLOVE OF GARLIC MINCED
- 1 BALL OF MOZZARELLA (BUFFALO WOULD BE BETTER)

READ SHOPPING LIST

DIRECTIONS

1. **Preheat** a nonstick pan
2. **Place** the zucchini in the pan and cook for a of couple minutes on each side, or until tender

1. **Toss** the tomatoes with chopped basil, minced garlic, salt, pepper and Extra Virgin Olive Oil
2. **Lay** 2 spoonfuls of the tomato cubes on the dish and bundle them up with the slices of the grilled zucchini
3. **Gently** use the blades of chives like a string for bundling up the zucchini
4. **Lay** the mozzarella on top and decorate with leaves of basil

PAPPA AL POMODORO

Bread tomatoes soup

TOTAL TIME: 45
PREP: 20
COOK: 40
LEVEL: easy

INGREDIENTS

MAKES 4 SERVINGS

- 2 CLOVES OF GARLIC
- 1 BUNCH OF BASIL
- 4 CUPS (1 LITER) VEGETABLE BROTH
- ABUNDANT EXTRA VIRGIN OLIVE OIL
- 10 OZ. (300 G) STALE TUSCAN BREAD*
- 1 RED CHILI PEPPER (FRESH OR DRY)
- 1 LB. (500 G) TOMATO SAUCE (SEE RECIPE)
- SALT AS REQUIRED
- *(ONLY TUSCAN BREAD-NO OTHER BREAD - BAGUETTE, CIABATTA, FOCACCIA ETC ... ARE UNSUITABLE FOR THIS RECIPE)

READ SHOPPING LIST

DIRECTIONS

1. **In** a large pot add the garlic (minced), the basil (chopped grossly), the red chili pepper (chopped) and the oil
2. **Cook** (medium - heat) untill the basil is lightly fried
3. **Add** the tomato sauce and a little bit of the salt
4. **After 8-10** minutes add the slices of bread and the broth
5. **Continue** simmering and mix until all the bread has absorbed as much liquid as possible, yielding a baby food-like consistency
6. **You** can serve warm or cold
7. **Adding** more basil or Extra Virgin Olive Oil if you like

NEVER PARMIGIANO OR ANY OTHER CHEESE

SECONDO

SFORMATO DI CARCIOFI CON CIPOLLINE AL BALSAMICO

Savory tart with artichokes served with onion and Balsamic

TOTAL TIME: 1,25 h
PREP: 35
COOK: 35
LEVEL: medium

INGREDIENTS

MAKES 4 SERVINGS

FOR THE SAVORY TART WITH ARTICHOKES
- 4-5 ARTICHOKES
- 1 TBSP OF FRESH THYME
- 1/2 GLASS OF EXTRA VIRGIN OLIVE OIL
- 1 CLOVE OF GARLIC
- 2 EGGS
- 35 OZ (100 G.) GRATED PARMIGIANO
- 5 OZ (150 G) FRESH RICOTTA
- BREAD CRUMBS
- BUTTER TO BASTE THE SOUFLEÉ DISHES
- 1-2 GLASSES OF WATER OR VEGETABLE BROTH (PREFERABLY WARM)

FOR THE GLAZED ONIONS WITH BALSAMIC
- 6-7 SMALL SWEET ONIONS PEELED PER PERSON
- 1,7 OZ (50 C.) BUTTER
- SALT AND PEPPER
- 3-4 TSBP OF BALSAMIC VINEGAR*
- *ORIGINAL FROM MODENA (DON'T USE GLAZE AND REDUCTIONS. IT ISN'T IMPORTANT TO USE THE EXPENSIVE "AGED" KIND)

READ SHOPPING LIST

DIRECTIONS

FOR THE SAVORY TART WITH ARTICHOKES
1. **Pull** off and discard tough outer leaves, starting with the outer ring and working your way around and in (keep going--pulling off and discarding leaves--as leaves turn tender and yellow)
2. **Cut** off and discard the crown of artichoke
3. **Use** scissors to cut off and discard the thorny tops
4. **Slice** the artichockes vertically about 1/4-inch thick
5. **Put** the artichokes, clean, in a basin of water acidulated to prevent the formation of black parts which, remember, must be eliminated
6. **In** a frying pan with a little oil, fry gently 1 clove of garlic (minced) and the thyme
7. **Then** add the sliced artichokes
8. **Add** salt, cover with a lid, lower the heat and cook (it will take 10-15 minutes)
9. **Preheat** the oven to 360° degrees F
10. **Meanwhile** beat the eggs
11. **Add** to the eggs the Parmigiano and the Ricotta cheese
12. **Mix** very well
13. **Add** the artichokes (when they are cold)
14. **Baste** the soufleé dishes with butter and the bread crumbs
15. **Add** them gently to the mixture
16. **Cook** until the savory tart is golden-brown and puffy

Serve with the glazed onions

FOR THE GLAZED ONIONS WITH BALSAMIC
1. **Steam** the onions (in the microwave for 10 minutes)
2. **Melt** the butter in a nonstick pan (cook over a low fire)
3. **Add** the steamed onions and the salt and pepper
4. **Cook** over a low fire for 20 minutes untill the onions become brown and soft
5. **Be** careful to not burn the onions. In the case that you do, add some warm water to them
6. **Take** them off the fire and add the Balsamic vinegar
7. **Warm** before serving

GELATO AL MASCARPONE E AMARETTI

Gelato with Mascarpone and Amaretto cookies

TOTAL TIME: 35
PREP: 10
COOK:
LEVEL: easy

INGREDIENTS

MAKES 4 SERVINGS

- 1 CUP *8 OZ.* (226 G.) MASCARPONE CHEESE ROOM TEMPERATURE)
- 4 EGG YOLKS
- 5 TBSP OF ICE SUGAR
- 1 CUP HEAVY CREAM
- 1/2 GLASS OF AMERETTO LIQUOR
- AMARETTI COOKIES
- COCOA POWDER

DIRECTIONS

1. **Whip** 4 egg yolks with sugar until stiff
2. **Add** the Amaretto liquor
3. **Fold** the mascarpone cheese into yolk mixture thus obtaining a soft cream
4. **Add** gently the heavy cream stirring
5. **Put** the mixture in a ice cream machine
6. **Put** the cups in the freezer (at least 30 minutes)
7. **When** the "gelato" will be ready (20-25 minutes) put in freezer for 10-15 minutes before to serving
8. **Put** quickly, the ice cream in your cups
9. **Dust** the top the cocoa powder using a sifter
10. **In** top add the Amaretti cookies

From My Florentine Kitchen

SUGGESTIONS

Variants for Caprese salad

INGREDIENTS

- 1 MEDIUM TOMATO PER PERSON
- 1 BOCCONCINO OF MOZZARELLA
- (ARE SMALL MOZZARELLA CHEESES THE SIZE OF AN EGG) PER PERSON
- BASIL
- 1 TBSP OF PESTO PER PERSON
- EXTRA VIRGIN OILIVE OIL
- SALT AND PEPPER

DIRECTIONS

1. **Cut** in two side the tomato and empty it with a spoon
2. **Drizzle** with salt, pepper and oil
3. **Lay** the bocconcino of mozzarella inside the tomato
4. **Add** the pesto and oil
5. **Cover** with the half of tomatoe
6. **You** can decore with chives, basil, add some drops of Balsamic...

INGREDIENTS

- 1 MEDIUM TOMATO PER PERSON
- 1 BOCCONCINO OF MOZZARELLA (ARE SMALL MOZZARELLA CHEESES THE SIZE OF AN EGG) PER PERSON
- CHIVES
- 1 TBSP OF DILL
- EXTRA VIRGIN OILIVE OIL
- SALT AND PEPPER

DIRECTIONS

1. **Cut** in cube the tomato
2. **Pour** in a stainer and drizzle with salt
3. **Wait** 10-15 minutes before to use (is important drain the water)
4. **Cut** the mozzarella in very thin slices
5. **Put** on top to any slice pepper and dill
6. **Tie** the slices of mozzrella with the 4 row chives crossed; as for tie a gift box.
7. **Lay** 1 or 2 spoons of cubes of tomatoes, dress with oil
8. **Lay** the "pack" of mozzarella the tomato
9. **Add** Oil in top

Menù N 6 Caterina

ANTIPASTO
White beans and tomatoes, toast
with black cabbage, roast sausage

PRIMO
Chickpeas Soup

SECONDO
Chicken with mushrooms

DOLCE
Blueberry tiramisu

FAGIOLI ALL'UCCELLETTO, SALSICCIA, CROSTINI AL CAVOLO NERO

White beans and tomatoes, toast with black cabbage, roast sausage

TOTAL TIME: 1 h
PREP: 30
COOK: 25
LEVEL: easy

INGREDIENTS

MAKES **4** SERVINGS

FAGIOLI ALL'UCCELLETTO
- **2 CLOVES** OF GARLIC
- **10 OZ (300 G) BEANS** (WHITE BEANS) CANNED OR COOKED *
- **1/2 CUP** EXTRA VIRGIN OLIVE OIL
- PEPPER
- **1/2 LB. (200 G.)** PEELED TOMATOES
- SALT
- **1 SPRIG** SAGE

* RECIPE FOR COOKING DRIED BEANS

READ SHOPPING LIST

TOAST WITH BLACK CABBAGE
- **SMALL** SLICES OF BREAD 1/4 INCH THICK
- **4 TBSP** OF COOKED WHITE BEANS
- **4 TBSP** EXTRA VIRGIN OLIVE OIL
- SALT AND PEPPER
- **4 LEAVES** OF BLACK CABBAGE* (COOKED, STEAMED OR BOILED - OR IN MICROWAVE)
- **2 TBSP** OF BREAD CRUMBS CHOPPED GROSSLY

READ SHOPPING LIST

DIRECTIONS

White beans and tomatoes
1. **In** a skillet heat the oil, garlic and sage (2-3 minutes)
2. **Add** the tomatoes and cook until the sauce is dense
3. **Add** the beans, salt and pepper and cook for 15 minutes

ROAST SAUSAGES
1. **Cut** the sausages into small pieces (2 inches)
2. **Roll** every piece with a sage leaf (use the toothpick to close them)
3. **Cook** on the nonstick skillet 2-3 minutes each side

TOAST WITH BLACK CABBAGE
1. **In** a nonstick skillet heat 1 tbsp of the oil.
2. **Add** the bread crumbs and cook for a few minutes (untill they become golden and crunchy)
3. **In** a bowl toss the beans with oil, salt and pepper
4. **Toast** the slices of bread
5. **As** soon as the bread is ready, top the slices with the cavolo nero, white beans and the crunchy bread crumbs

ROAST SAUSAGES
- **2 SAUSAGES** (BREAKFAST SAUSAGE)
- **8 LEAVES** OF SAGE
- **8 TOOTHPICKS**
- PEPPER

READ SHOPPING LIST

From My Florentine Kitchen

VELLUTATA DI CECI

Chickpeas Soup

TOTAL TIME: 30
PREP: 10
COOK: 30
LEVEL: easy

INGREDIENTS

MAKES 4 SERVINGS

- 1 LB. CHICKPEAS (STEAMED OR 2 CANNEDS)
- HALF WHITE ONION
- HALF A CARROT
- HALF A STICK OF CELERY
- 1 OR 2 CLOVES OF GARLIC
- 1 TBSB OF ROSEMARY (MINCED)
- SALT AND PEPPER
- 4-6 CUPS HOT WATER AND STOCK CUBE OR VEGETABLE BROTH
- 4 TBSP EXTRA VIRGIN OLIVE OIL
- TRUFFLE OIL FOR TOSSING

DIRECTIONS

1. **Chop** onion, celery, garlic and carrot (medium size)
2. **In** a skillet heat the oil
3. **Add** the mix of vegetables and the rosemary
4. **Cook** until the vegetables are golden (not burned!) 10-13 minutes
5. **Add** the chickpeas
6. **Cook**, stir some times, for 10 minutes
7. **Add** salt and pepper
8. **Blend** with hand mixer, until you have a cream (pouree)
9. **Add** the hot water and stock cube or vegetable stock (keeping the hand mixer in action) until you have the preferred consistency
10. **Serve** with truffle oil

READ SHOPPING LIST

From My Florentine Kitchen

SECONDO

POLLO AI FUNGHI

Chicken with mushrooms

TOTAL TIME: 40
PREP: 15
COOK: 30
LEVEL: easy

INGREDIENTS

MAKES 4 SERVINGS

- **8 BONELESS**, SKINLESS CHICKEN LEGS
- **CORN STARCH** (TO FLOUR THE CHICKEN)
- **2 TBSP** EXTRA VIRGIN OLIVE OIL
- **2 TBSP** BUTTER
- **1 LB.** OF MIXED MUSHROOMS, WIPED CLEAN AND SLICED 1/2-INCH-THICK*
- **1 GARLIC** CLOVE, MINCED
- **1 CARROT** IN CUBE
- **1 STEAK** OF CELLERY IN CUBE
- **2 TBSP** CHOPPED FRESH FLAT-LEAF PARSLEY OR THYME
- **SALT AND PEPPER**

* PORTOBELLO MUSHROOMS, STEMS AND CAPS SEPARATED
WHITE MUSHROOMS
SHIITAKE MUSHROOMS,
OYSTER MUSHROOMS, TRIMMED AND HALVED LENGTHWISE IF LARGE
DRY PORCINI

READ SHOPPING LIST

DIRECTIONS

1. **In** a nonstick skillet heat the oil and butter
2. **Add** the carrot and celery
3. **Add** the chicken and coat both sides with corn starch
4. **Transfer** the chicken to the skillet; saute until cooked through, about 3-4 minutes per side
5. **Add** the mushrooms, the thyme, parsley and garlic
6. **Cover** with lid and cook for a few minutes (the mushrooms leave the water so no need to add broth or water. In case the mushroom's water will be insufficient add a warm water)
7. **Leave** the lid and cook stirring until the mushrooms are cooked
8. **Add salt and pepper**
9. **Serve** the chicken, topped with the mushrooms

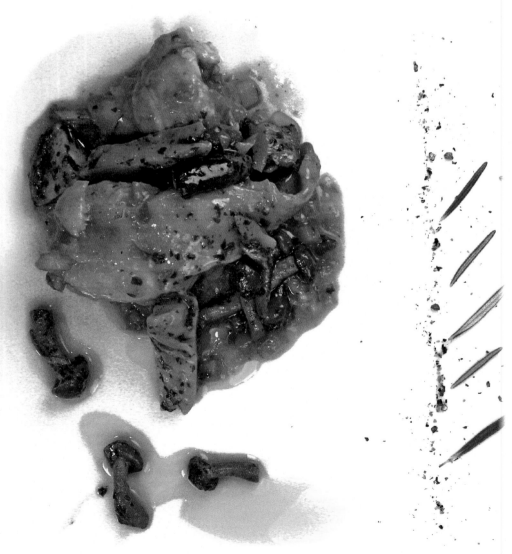

From My Florentine Kitchen 42

TIRAMISU AI FRUTTI DI BOSCO

Blueberry tiramisu

TOTAL TIME: 25
PREP: 15
COOK: 0
LEVEL: easy

INGREDIENTS

MAKES 4 SERVINGS

- 1 CUP *8 OZ.* (226 G.) MASCARPONE CHEESE (ROOM TEMPERATURE)
- 3 EGGS
- 4 TBSP OF SUGAR
- PINCH OF SALT
- 12 LADYFINGERS FOR DECORATIONS (OPTIONAL)
- 7 OZ. (200 G.) SPONGE CAKE.
- 1 CUP BLUEBERRY SYRUP
- 3 TBSP WATER
- 2 CUPS WITH MIXED BARRIES

READ SHOPPING LIST

DIRECTIONS

HOW TO MAKE THE BASIC CREAM

1. **With** an electric mixer, beat the egg whites until stiff. Add a pinch of salt and 1 Tbsp of sugar while mixing
2. **In** a separate bowl, beat the egg yolks, adding 3 Tbsp of sugar. Beat until the mixture has a consistency of mousse (about 3-4 minutes)
3. **Add** the mascarpone cheese to the egg yolk mixture. Beat quickly at a reduced speed until creamy. Using a wooden spoon, fold in the egg whites

HOW TO MAKE THE TIRAMISÙ

4. **In** a separate bowl combine a cup of blueberry syrup and 3 Tbsp of water for dipping
5. **Cut** Sponge Cake into vertical slices exactly 1/4 inch thick. You can use the small pieces to fill in any gaps
6. **With** a pastry brush moisten the sponge cake with the blueberry syrup
7. **For** this dessert use one of the following containers: 9x9 cake pan (glass, plastic, ceramic, alluminium): Glasses (8 or more Fl. Oz.): Bowls (8-12 Fl. Oz.) place a layer of the "Basic cream", and then the sponge cake soaked in a blueberry syrup. Repeat for 2 layers.
8. **Optional:** Serve on the plate and decorate with Ladyfingers and forest fruits
9. **Chill** at least 2-3 hours before serving

From My Florentine Kitchen

SUGGESTIONS

A FEW WORDS ABOUT MUSHROOMS

The mushrooms most familiar to U.S. buyers are the "whites," or common button agaricus.

Other varieties of agaricus, the criminis and portabellas, are known as the "browns." Shiitake (shee tah kay), oyster, wood ear and enoki (e nok e) mushrooms are also popular.

Particularly in the Pacific Northwest and the northeastern United States, seasonal species such as morels, oysters and chanterelles are gathered in the wild and sold at farmers' markets and through retail stores.

California and New Mexico in the US are major hotspots for Porcini gathering, with large harvests available in the pine forests and mountain areas.

You're more likely to see dried porcini at the grocery store than fresh.

To prepare dried Porcini steep them in boiling water to cover until they are reconstituted. After draining the Porcini mince, them but keep the steeping liquid. This liquid adds even more concentrated Porcini flavor to the recipe, just make sure you strain it first.

HOW TO CLEAN THE MUSHROOMS!

AREN'T DIRTY....DON'T WASH THEM... RUB EACH ONE INDIVIDUALLY WITH A CLEAN PAPER TOWEL

THEY ARE VERY DIRTY....(DEBRIS, LITTLE CRITTERS ....) RINSE.....

BUT NEVER SOAK THEM!

ANYWAY ... DRY THEM WELL AND COOK THEM SOON AFTER.

IN PLACE OF CHICKEN ...LAMB!

INGREDIENTS

*   8 LAMB RIBS
*   CORN STARCH (TO FLOUR THE RIBS)
*   2 TBSP EXTRA VIRGIN OLIVE OIL
*   2 TBSP BUTTER
*   1 LB. OF MIXED MUSHROOMS, WIPED CLEAN AND SLICED 1/2-INCH-THICK*
*   1 GARLIC CLOVE, MINCED
*   1 CARROT IN CUBE
*   1 STEAK OF CELLERY IN CUBE
*   1 TBSP CHOPPED FRESH THYME
*   1 TBSP CHOPPED FRESH ROSEMARY
*   SALT AND PEPPER
*   2 GLASSES OF RED WINE

DIRECTIONS

1. **In** a nonstick skillet heat the oil and butter
2. **Add** the carrot and celery
3. **Add** the lamb and coat both sides with corn starch
4. **Transfer** the lamb to the skillet; saute until cooked through, about 5-6 minutes per side
5. **Add** the red wine
6. **Wait** untill is completely evaporated
7. **Add** the mushrooms, the thyme, rosemary and garlic
8. **Cook** stirring until the mushrooms are cooked
9. **Add** salt and pepper
10. **Serve** the lamb with the mushrooms

Menu' N 7 Dante

ANTIPASTO
Small bruschette with chicken paté and ...

PRIMO
Ricotta dumplings with cherry tomatoes and basil

SECONDO
Tenderloin pork in crust with Balsamic

DOLCE
"Frozen Ricotta" with mix berries and Balsamic

Crostini con patè di pollo e ...

Small bruschette with chicken paté and ......

TOTAL TIME: 35
PREP: 15
COOK: 20
LEVEL: easy

INGREDIENTS

MAKES 4 SERVINGS

- **8 OZ (230 G)** UNSALTED BUTTER, SOFTENED
- **1/2 LB (250 G)** CHICKEN BREAST, TRIMMED
- **1 SHALLOT,** FINELY CHOPPED
- **1 CARROT** CUT INTO CUBES
- **1 STICK** CELERY CUT INTO CUBES
- **1 TBSP** SOFT THYME LEAVES
- **1 CLOVE** GARLIC, FINELY CHOPPED
- **1/2 GLASS** OF BRANDY OR SIMILAR
- **1 CUP** OF VEGETABLE STOCK
- SALT AND PEPPER
- **SMALL** SLICES OF BREAD 1/4 INCH THICK

DIRECTIONS

1. **Heat** 1 oz. (30 G) of the butter in a frying pan until foaming
2. **Add** the carrot, celery, thyme and celery
3. **Cook** for 5-7 minutes or until golden-brown
4. **Add** the chicken breast and fry for 10 minutes, or until golden-brown and cooked through
5. **Add** the Brandy and simmer until the alcohol evaporates, about 3-5 minutes
6. **Place** the mixture in a food processor including the remaining butter
7. **Blend** until smooth
8. **Cover** with plastic wrap, cool then refrigerate.
   If it will not be used within 48 hours,
   cover the top with clarified butter
9. **Toast** the slices of bread
10. **As** soon as the toast is
    ready, top them with the chicken paté

READ SHOPPING LIST

GNOCCHI DI RICOTTA CON POMODORINI E BASILICO

Ricotta dumplings with cherry tomatoes and basil

TOTAL TIME: 25
PREP: 15
COOK: 5
LEVEL: easy

INGREDIENTS

MAKES 4 SERVINGS

- 1/2 LB. (250 G.) OF FRESH RICOTTA
- 1 CUP ALL-PURPOSE FLOUR, PLUS EXTRA FOR ROLLING OUT THE GNOCCHI (DUMPLINGS)
- 1/4 POUND FRESHLY GRATED PARIMIGIANO CHEESE PLUS 1 TBSP PER PERSON FOR SAVORED
- 1 EGG
- SALT AND PEPPER
- PINCH OF NUTMEG (OPTIONAL)
- 1 TBSP BUTTER PER PERSON (MELT)

DIRECTIONS

1. **Drain** the ricotta
2. **Transfer** to a large bowl and add the flour, Parmigiano cheese, egg, pinch of nutmeg and ground black pepper
3. **Mix** until completely combined and it has made a relatively firm dough; if you need more flour to reach that point, add it in small amounts until it holds together
4. **Dust** a work surface with flour (a tray or big plate covered with baking paper)
5. **Prepare the dumplings:**
6. **With** your hands make the small balls (use one Tbsp of mixture for any single dumpling)
7. **Repeat** with the remaining mixture to make gnocchi
8. **Put** the tray with the dumplings in a refrigerator for a minimum of a half hour
9. **Bring** a large pot of salted water to a boil, then reduce the heat to maintain a gentle simmer
10. **Add** the gnocchi to the simmering water in two batches and cook until they float, about 2 minutes
11. **Using** a slotted spoon or spider, drain each briefly to gently shake off any excess water, and transfer to the dish in a single layer
12. **Toss** sauce with toamtoes and basil.*

READ SHOPPING LIST

From My Florentine Kitchen

FILETTO DI MAIALE IN SFOGLIA CON BALSAMICO

Tenderloin pork in crust with Balsamic

TOTAL TIME: 35
PREP: 15
COOK: 25
LEVEL: easy

INGREDIENTS

MAKES 4 SERVINGS

- 1 PORK TENDERLOIN
  (ABOUT 1 POUND)
- 2 TBSP OF EXTRA VIRGIN OLIVE OIL
- 1/2 CUP CHOPPED THYME,
  ROSEMARY AND SAGE
- 1 OR 2 CLOVE GARLIC (MINCHED)
- SALT AND PEPPER
- 1 PIECE (1/2 LB.) OF FROZEN PUFF
  PASTRY
- 1 YOLK BEATEN
- BALSAMIC VINEGAR
  (1 TBSP PER PERSON)

READ SHOPPING LIST

DIRECTIONS

1. **Season** the tenderloin with salt, pepper, garlic and mix of herbs
2. **In** a large sauce pan, heat 3 tablespoons of olive oil
3. **When** the oil is hot, sear the tenderloin for 2 to 3 minutes on all sides
4. **Remove** from the pan and cool
5. **Preheat** the oven to 350° degrees F
6. **Lay** the seared tenderloin in the center of the puff pastry
7. **Wrap** the tenderloin in the puff pastry, tucking the sides in completely
8. **Brush** the entire puff pastry with the yolk and place on a baking sheet (with baking paper).
9. **Bake** for about 20 to 25 minutes for medium rare, or until the pastry is golden brown
10. **Remove** the roll from the oven and allow to rest for 10 minutes before serving
11. **Serve** with a drizzle of Balsamic

GELATO DI RICOTTA CON FRUTTI DI BOSCO AL BALSAMICO

"Frozen Ricotta" with mix berries and Balsamic

TOTAL TIME: 45
PREP: 15
COOK: 40
LEVEL: easy

INGREDIENTS

MAKES 4 SERVINGS

- 1 LB. (500 G) OF MIX BERRY CLEAN
- 5 TBSP ICE-SUGAR
- 10 OZ. (300 G.) FRESH RICOTTA (THE SWEETER THE YOU CAN FIND)
- 1/2 CUP HEAVY CREAM
- 3 TBSP BALSAMIC

DIRECTIONS

1. In a pot put the mix of berry and 4 Tbsp of ice sugar
2. At low heat cook for 30-40 minutes stirring sometimes
3. When is done, turn off the fire and add the Balsamic

1. In bowl (stainless steel) mix ricotta with a spoon of ice sugar and cream
2. If you have a Ice cream maker you can use it, otherwise you can put the bowl in a freezer and stir every 10 minutes untill is done!
3. Pour 2-3 Tbsp of the berries with a "Balsamic sirup" on the dish and add the "frozen ricotta"

READ SHOPPING LIST

From My Florentine Kitchen

SUGGESTIONS

DUMPLINGS WITH SAUCE WITH RADICCHIO AND ONION (RED SALAD)

INGREDIENTS

* 1 LB. (500 G) RED SALAD
* 1 MEDIUM ONION
* 2 TBSP BUTTER
* 2-3 TBSP EXTRAVIRGIN OILVE OIL
* SALT PEPPER

DIRECTIONS

1. **Cut** in a strips the salad (strips thikness half inch)
2. **Cut** the onion in a slices very thin
3. **In** a saucepan melt the butter an oil
4. **Add** the onion and cook low heat, for 5-7 minutes
5. **Add** the strips of salad and cook for 5-7 minutes (untill the salad will be completly cooked)
6. **Add** salt and pepper

DUMPLINGS WITH PESTO AND FONDUE

INGREDIENTS

* **PREPARE** THE PESTO (SEE THE RECIPE PAGE)
* 1/4 OF LB. CHEESES. YOU CAN USE ANY QUALITY OF SOFT CHEESES THAT YOU LIKE

DIRECTIONS

1. **In** a "double saucepan" melt, with 2-3 Tbsp of milk, the cheeses.
2. **Stir** well
3. **Lay** on the dish (better a warm dish) 1 or 2 Tbsp of fondue
4. **Add** the dumplings and toss with pesto
5. **Eat quickly!**

THE MUSHROOMS... IN TOP OF TENDERLOIN

INGREDIENTS

* 1 LB. OF MIX OF MUSHROOMS (PORTOBELLO, CREMINI, PORCINI ALSO DRY) CUT AND CLEAN
* 1-2 CLOVES OF GARLIC MINCED
* BUNCH OF PARSLEY MINCED OR 1 TBSP OF FRESH THYME MINCED
* 2-3 TBSP EXTRA VIRGIN OLIVE OIL
* SALT

DIRECTIONS

1. **In** a large saucepan, medium heat, put the garlic and the parsely or thyme
2. **When** start to sizzle add the mushrooms
3. **Cook** stirring untill the mushrooms are not done (medium/hight heat)
4. **In** the end add the salt
5. **Lay** the slice of tenderloin on the dish and put in top 2-3 Tbsp of mushrooms

Menù N 8 Machiavelli

ANTIPASTO
Pie Savory with vegetables and feta

PRIMO
Pumpkin Soup

SECONDO
Chicken "Saltimbocca"

DOLCE
Cream with Apricots in Rosemary Syrup

TORTA SALATA DI VERDURE CON FETA

Pie Savory with vegetables and feta

TOTAL TIME: 1,40
PREP: 20
COOK: 45
LEVEL: easy

INGREDIENTS

MAKES 4 SERVINGS

- 1 PIECE (1/2 LB.) OF FROZEN PUFF PASTRY
- 1 ZUCCHINA
- 1 MEDIUM EGGPLANT
- 2 RIPE TOMATOES (MEDIUM SIZE) CUT IN CUBE
- 1 ONION (MEDIUM)
- FRESH BASIL (SMALL BUNCH) CHOPPED GROSSLY
- BIT OF RED CHILLY
- SALT
- 5-6 TBSP EXTRAVIRGIN OLIVE OIL
- 1/2 LB. (250 G.) FETA CHEESE
- 1 YOLK

READ SHOPPING LIST

DIRECTIONS

1. **Defrost** the puff pastry
2. **Cut** the Eggplant in cube
3. **Cut** the Zucchina in cube
4. **Cut** the onion in thin slices
5. **In** a saucepan medium heat add the Oil and after 1 minute add the onion
6. **Cook** for 2-3 minutes
7. **Add** the vegetables (egglapnt, zucchina and tomatoes) and salt
8. **Cover** with lid and at low/medium heat cook, stirring, until the vegetables begin to be soft (15-20 minutes)
9. **Add** the basil, red chilly
10. **Cool** down
11. **Unroll** the puff pastry and place it in a Plum cake mold (covered with paper bake)
12. **Make** a first layer of mix vegetable
13. **Add** a second layers of Feta cheeses and finish with a layer of mix vegetable
14. **Close** the puff pastry
15. **Brush** the entire puff pastry with the yolk
16. **Bake** (356 F) 25-35 minutes

WAIT 30 MINUTES BEFORE TO SERVE

ZUPPA DI ZUCCA

Pumpkin Soup

TOTAL TIME: 45
PREP: 15
COOK: 40
LEVEL: easy

INGREDIENTS

MAKES 4 SERVINGS

- 4 TBSP OF BUTTER
- 5-6 TBSP EXTRA VIRGIN OLIVE OIL
- 1 ONION, CHOPPED
- 1 CARROT, CHOPPED
- 1 STICK OF CELERY CHOPPED
- 1 LB. OF PUMPKIN, DICED
- 3 CUPS VEGETABLE STOCK OR 1 STOCK CUBE AND 3 CUPS OF WATER
- SALT AND FRESHLY GROUND PEPPER

DIRECTIONS

1. **In** a stockpot over medium heat, melt butter and oil, add the onion, carrot, celery and pumpkin
2. **Cook** until all are tender, about 20-25 minutes covered with lid (stir)
3. **Puree** the mixture with hand mixer
4. **Add** the stock (or the stock cube and 3 cups of warm water) and simmer for 10 minutes (keeping the hand mixer in action) until you have the preferred consistency
5. **Season**, to taste, with salt and pepper

READ SHOPPING LIST

From My Florentine Kitchen

SALTIMBOCCA DI POLLO

Chicken "Saltimbocca"

TOTAL TIME: 40
PREP: 20
COOK: 10
LEVEL: easy

INGREDIENTS

MAKES 4 SERVINGS

- **8** THINLY SLICED CHICKEN BREAST ABOUT 1/4-INCH THICK
- **8** THINLY SLICES OF PARMA HAM OR SIMILAR
- **8** FRESH SAGE LEAVES, PLUS MORE FOR GARNISH
- CORN STARCH, FOR DREDGING
- SALT AND FRESHLY GROUND BLACK PEPPER
- **2 TBSP** EXTRA-VIRGIN OLIVE OIL
- **2 TBSP** UNSALTED BUTTER
- **2 TBSP** DRY WHITE WINE
- **1/4 CUP** WATER

____ **8** TOOTHPICKS
STEAK HAMMER OR MEAT TENDERIZE

DIRECTIONS

1. **Place** a piece of plastic wrap below and on top of a slice of chicken and flatten using smooth side of meat mallot, working from middle to edges, until 1/4 inch thick. Set aside and repeat until all the chicken has been flattened
1. **Lay** a piece of prosciutto on top of each slice of chicken and lay one sage leaf in the center of each cutlet and wrap them
2. **Weave** a toothpick in and out of the chicken to secure the prosciutto and sage
3. **Dredge** the chicken in the corn starch, shaking off the excess
4. **Heat** the oil and butter in a large skillet over a medium flame
5. **Put** the "chicken wrapped" in the pan
6. **Cook** for 3-4 minutes to crisp it up and then flip the chicken over and saute the other side for 2 minutes, until golden
7. **Add** the wine, stirring and let the wine cook down for a minute to burn off some of the alcohol
8. **Season** with salt and pepper
9. **Pour** the sauce over the saltimbocca, garnish with sage leaves and serve immediately

READ SHOPPING LIST

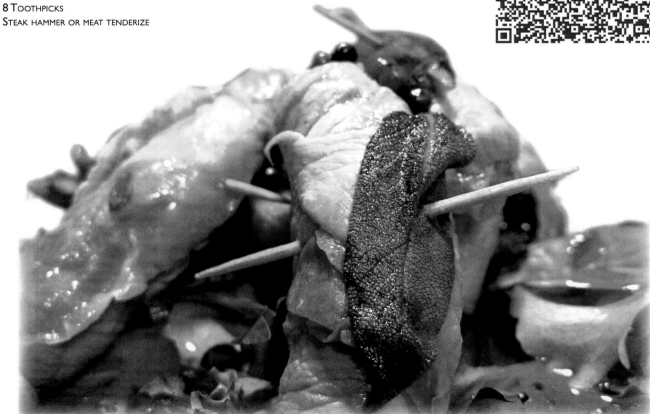

CREMA CON ALBICOCCHE IN SCIROPPO DI ROSMARINO

Cream with Apricots in Rosemary Syrup

TOTAL TIME: 40
PREP: 15
COOK: 20
LEVEL: easy

INGREDIENTS

MAKES 4 SERVINGS

- 1 CUP 8 OZ. (226 G.) MASCARPONE CHEESE ROOM TEMPERATURE)
- 4 EGG YOLKS
- 8 TBSP OF ICE SUGAR
- 12 APRICOT (PITTED AND CUT IN FOUR)
- 1 CUP OF WATER
- 2-3 BRANCHES OF ROSEMARY

DIRECTIONS

1. **Pour** the sugar in a water
2. **To** bring a boil
3. **Add** the rosemary
4. **Cook**, stirring for 15-20 minutes
5. **Add** the apricots
6. **Turn** off the heat
7. **Leave** the syrup with the apricots to cool

PREPARE THE CREAM
8. **Whip** 4 egg yolks with sugar until stiff
9. **Fold** the mascarpone cheese into yolk mixture
10. **In** top add the the aprictos with Rosemary syrup

READ SHOPPING LIST

From My Florentine Kitchen

SUGGESTIONS

...Pie savory... without puff pastry!
SAVORY TART WITH GRILLED VEGETABLE AND HAM

INGREDIENTS
- 1 PIECE (1/2 LB.) OF FROZEN PUFF PASTRY
- 2 ZUCCHINA
- 2 MEDIUM EGGPLANTS
- 2 RIPE TOMATOES (MEDIUM SIZE) CUT IN CUBE
- FRESH BASIL (SMALL BUNCH) CHOPPED GROSSLY
- 6-8 SLICES OF HAM
- BIT OF RED CHILLY
- SALT
- 5-6 TBSP EXTRAVIRGIN OLIVE OIL
- 1 YOLK

DIRECTIONS
1. **Defrost** the puff pastry
2. **Cut** lengthwise into 1/4-inch strips the zucchina and eggplant and grill
3. **Cut** the tomatoes in cube put the salt and pour in a sieve for drain
4. **Unroll** the puff pastry and place it in a Plum cake mold (covered with paper bake)
5. **Make** a first layer with zucchini, bit of Oil, salt, basil and tomatoes
6. **Add** the ham to cover the layer (one or two slices)
7. **Make** a later layer with eggpant bit of Oil, salt, basil and tomatoes
8. **Repeat** untill the ingredients are finished
9. **Close** the puff pastry
10. **Brush** the entire puff pastry with the yolk
11. **Bake (356 F)** 25-35 minutes
12. **Wait 30** minutes before to serve

Baked leek ....for the pamkin soup!

INGREDIENTS
- 1 LEEK
- 2-3 TBSP EXTRA VIRGIN OLIVE OIL
- 4-5 TBSP GRATED PARMIGIANO

DIRECTIONS
1. **Cut** lengthwise the leek in two part
2. **Divide** the leaves cut the "green"
3. **Cut** in small strips every leaf (as a fringe edge)
4. **Lay** on the sheet of paper bake the leek and with a brush spread the oil on it.
5. **Dust** with Parmigiano
6. **Bake** for 15-20 minutes (untill is golden-brown) 365 F°
7. **Put** in top of soup

SALTIMBOCCA (JUMP IN THE MOUTH)

The original recipe want the Veal not the chicken.
You can also decide to don't wrap the meat. The result will be like a scoloppini with slice of ham and sage.
Anywy is a great, easy and flavored dish that you can prpare in few minutes!

Menù N 9 Firenze

ANTIPASTO
Mango Potatoes and prawn
zuppa
Veloutes Cream of white beans
with shrimp and Pancetta

PRIMO
Pasta with mussels and roast
tomatoes

SECONDO
Sea bass with cherry tomatoes,
black olives and raw artichokes

DOLCE
Lemon sorbet

Insalata di mango, patate e gamberi

Mango Potatoes and prawn

Total Time: 25
Prep: 15
Cook: 25
Level: easy

DIRECTIONS

1. **Cut** every prawn in two o three parts
2. **If** you like you can steamed the prawn just 1-2 minutes
3. **In** a bowl mix all ingredients: potatoes, mango, garlic, salt, red chilly, fresh dill and prawns
4. **Stir** and add the Extravirgin Olive Oil
5. **Serve** room temperature

INGREDIENTS

Makes **4** servings

- **2 Medium** potatoes (steamed and cut in cube)
- **1 Mango** peeled and cut in cube
- **8-10** prawns (fresh and cleaned)
- **1 Clove** of garlic minced
- **Pinch** of red chilly pepper
- **Extravirgin Olive oil**
- **Bunch** of fresh dill
- **Salt**

Read Shopping list

VELLUTATA DI CANNELLINI CON GAMBERI E PANCETTA

Veloutes Cream of white beans with shrimp and Pancetta

TOTAL TIME: 45
PREP: 20
COOK: 30
LEVEL: easy

INGREDIENTS

MAKES 4 SERVINGS

- 5 TBSP EXTRAVIRGIN OLIVE OIL
- 1 SHALLOTS, CHOPPED
- 2 (15-OUNCE) CANS CANNELLINI BEANS, DRAINED AND RINSED
- 4 CUPS VEGETAL BROTH OR 4 CUPS OF HOT WATER AND 1 STOCK CUBE
- 1/2 TEASPOON BLACK PEPPER
- 1 TEASPOON OF CHOP ROSEMARY
- TRUFFLE OIL, FOR DRIZZLING (OPTIONAL)
- 3 - 4 PRAWN TAILS PER PERSON - RAW AND FRESH - (AS WELL USE ALSO LOBSTER OR SHRIMPS)
- 3 - 4 SLICES BACON PER PRAWN TAILS (VERY THIN SLICES)

READ SHOPPING LIST

DIRECTIONS

1. **In** a soup pot add the olive oil and shallot
2. **Cook** until the shallots are softened (3-5 minutes)
3. **Add** the beans and rosemary stir to combine cook for 10-15 minutes
4. **Puree** the soup
5. **Add** the stock or the hot water with a stock cube until smooth
6. **Add** the salt
7. **Sieve** the soup with Chinois (a very fine sieve for the finest, lightest results)
8. **Wrap** the prawn tails with bacon
9. **Lay** on a oven plate with bake paper
10. **Grill** just for 2 - 3 minutes (just the bacon has to be crispy, not the prawn)
11. **Serve** the soup with prawn and bacon, drizzly with truffle oil and freshly ground black pepper

From My Florentine Kitchen

PASTA CON LE COZZE E POMODORINI ARROSTO

Pasta with mussels and roast tomatoes

TOTAL TIME: 30
PREP: 20
COOK: 20
LEVEL: easy

INGREDIENTS

MAKES 4 SERVINGS

- 4 POUNDS MUSSELS, SCRUBBED
- 1/4 CUP EXTRA-VIRGIN OLIVE OIL
- 4 CLOVES GARLIC, COARSELY CHOPPED
- 1/2 BUNCH ITALIAN PARSLEY, LEAVES FINELY CHOPPED
- SALT AND PINCH OF RED CHILLY PEPPER
- 1/2 POUND PAPPARDELLE

FOR A ROASTED TOMATOES
- 4-5 CHERRY TOMATOES PER PERSON
- 1 TBSP FRESH THYME CHOPPED
- SALT AND PEPPER
- 5-6 TBSP EXTRAVIRGIN OLIVE OIL

READ SHOPPING LIST

DIRECTIONS

1. **In** a large pan place the extravirgin olive oil, parsley, garlic and red chilly pepper cook for 2-3 minutes over high heat
2. **Add** mussels and cook, stirring frequently (covered) until all the mussels have opened (10 minutes)

FOR ROASTED TOMATOES
1. **Cut** the tomatoes in two
2. **Heat** the oil with the thyme
3. **Add** the tomatoes salt and pepper
4. **Cook** the tomatoes in both side untill are well done (10-12 minutes)
5. **Cook** pasta in boiling water until it is almost cooked through
6. **Drain** the pasta and add to the mussels and the roast tomatoes
7. **Serve** immediately

FILETTO DI BRANZINO CON POMODORINI, OLIVE E CARCIOFI

Sea bass with cherry tomatoes, black olives and raw artichokes

TOTAL TIME: 40
PREP: 20
COOK: 15
LEVEL: easy

INGREDIENTS

MAKES 4 SERVINGS

- 1 LB. (500 G) SEA BASS FILLET (WITHOUT BONES) CUT IN 5 PARTS (SAME SIZES)
- 1 LB. (500 G) CERRY TOMATOES
- 1 CUPS BLACK OLIVES (WITHOUT BONES)
- 2 CLEAN ARTICHOKES (CUT IN VERY THIN SLICES) SEE PAG. FOR TRIM THE ARTICHOCKES
- 5-6 TBSP EXTRAVIRGIN OLIVE OIL
- 1 TBSP FRESH THYME MINCED
- 1/2 GLASS WHITE DRY WINE
- SALT AND PEPPER

DIRECTIONS

1. **Cut** the cherry tomatoes in two
2. **Heat** the oil in a medium/large skillet over a medium flame
3. **Add** the tomatoes and black olives
4. **Cook** for 10 minutes stirring low flame
5. **Add** the sea bass
6. **Cook** 3-4 minutes for side
7. **Add** the thyme
8. **Add** the Wine and evaporate
9. **Adjust** sal and pepper
10. **Serve** with the raw artichokes in top
11. **Drizzle** with Extra Virgin Olive Oil, salt and pepper

READ SHOPPING LIST

From My Florentine Kitchen

Sorbetto al Pompelmo rosa
Pink Grapefruit sorbet

Total Time: 10
Prep: 20
Cook: 0
Level: easy

INGREDIENTS

Makes 4 servings

- 1 quarter (250 ml) of Pink grapefruit juice
- 2 Cups (250 g) of sugar
- 1 Pinch of salt
- 1 + half Cup (350 ml) of milk
- 2 White of eggs beaten (firm)
- Some red currant for decoration

Read Shopping list

DIRECTIONS

1. **With** hand mixer melt the sugar, pinch of salt with the juice and the milk
2. **Add** gently the white eggs beaten
3. **Insert** the mixture in a Ice-cream machine
4. **Work** untill is compact but soft
5. **If** you don't have the ice-cream machine, pour the mixture in a stinless steel bowl and put in freezer
6. **Stir** every 10-15 minutes

Menù N 10 Raffaello

ANTIPASTO **ZUPPA**
Mousse of Parmigiano cheese Mushrooms Soup

SECONDO **DOLCE**
Stuffed Zucchini Coffee Cream

MOUSSE DI PARMIGIANO

Mousse of Parmigiano cheese

TOTAL TIME: 15
PREP: 15
COOK: 0
LEVEL: easy

INGREDIENTS

MAKES 4 SERVINGS

- 3 EGGS
- 3,5 oz. (100G) GRATED PARMIGIANO
- 8,4 oz. FL (1/4 LITER) FRESH HEAVY CREAM
- BALSAMIC
- SALAD FOR SERVE

DIRECTIONS

1. **In** a food processor or with electric whisk beat the 3 yolks and the Parmigiano
2. **Beat** until became very creamy
3. **In** a bowl beat the white of eggs untill is stiff
4. **In** a bowl whip with a whisk the cream
5. **Gently** add the white eggs to the mixture with Parmigiano and the cream
6. **Put** in refrigerator for 1 hours
7. **Use** a pastry bag for lay on the dish or simply a spoon
8. **Add** in top a Tbsp of Balsamic and serve with mix salad

READ SHOPPING LIST

ZUPPA DI FUNGHI

Mushrooms Soup

TOTAL TIME: 45
PREP: 20
COOK: 40
LEVEL: easy

INGREDIENTS

MAKES **4** SERVINGS

- **5** OZ (140 G) FRESH SHIITAKE MUSHROOMS
- **5** OZ (140 G) FRESH PORTOBELLO MUSHROOMS
- **5** OZ (140 G) FRESH CREMINI (OR PORCINI) MUSHROOMS
- **4** TBSP EXTRAVIRGIN OLIVE OIL
- **1/4** POUND (1 STICK) PLUS
- **1** TBSP BUTTER
- **1** SCALLION OR 1 CUPS CHOPPED LEEKS
- **1** SMALL CARROT (CHOPPED)
- **2** CLOVES OF GARLIC (MINCED)
- **1** TBSP MINCED THYME
- **1** TBSP MINCED FRESH FLAT-LEAF PARSLEY
- SALT
- 1 PINCH RED CHILLY PEPPER
- 4-6 CUPS VEGETABLE BROTH

DIRECTIONS

1. **Clean** the mushrooms by wiping them with a dry paper towel. Don't wash them (if you can)!
2. **Chop** the mushroom and stems. Slice the caps 1/4-inch thick
3. **Heat** the olive oil and the butter in a large pot
4. **Add** the chopped the scallion or leek, carrot, the thyme and parsley and garlic
5. **Cook** over low heat for some minutes (5-7), until the begin to golden
6. **Add** the sliced mushroom cook for 10 minutes and stir
7. **Add** the vegetable broth, sal and red chilly pepper
8. **Reduce** the heat and simmer for 30 minutes

ZUCCHINE RIPIENE

Stuffed Zucchini

TOTAL TIME: 1,30 h
PREP: 35
COOK: 45
LEVEL: medium

INGREDIENTS

MAKES 4 SERVINGS

- 4 SPHERICAL ZUCCHINE (1 PER PERSON)
- 12 SLICES OF TOAST BREAD (WHITE OR WHOLE)
- 1 EGG
- 1 CUP GRATED PARMIGIANO
- 1 SMALL ONION OR 1 SHALLOT
- 2 RIPE TOMATOES (MEDIUM SIZE)
- 1 GLASS OF MILK
- 4-5 TBSP EXTRAVIRGIN OLIVE OIL
- 1 TBSP FRESH MINCED PARSLEY
- SALT AND PEPPER

DIRECTIONS

1. **Heat** the oven to 425 degrees F
2. **Cut** the zucchina and scoop out the soft center flesh with a spoon to produce a set of shallow shells to hold the stuffing
3. **Steam** the zucchine for 5-7 minutes
4. **Chop** the soft center of zucchina
5. **Heat** the extra-virgin olive oil in a skillet over medium-high heat and saute the onion or shallot for 5 minutes
6. **Add** in the soft part of zucchini chopped and tomatoes, season with salt, pepper and parsley and heat through for 7-8 minutes, then remove from the heat
7. **Soak** the bread in a milk untill becomes very soft
8. **Add** the bread to the mixture with zucchini and stir
9. **Add** the egg and Parmigiano
10. **Place** some of the filling inside each of the hollowed-out zucchini and bake at 425 degrees for about 30-40 minutes

READ SHOPPING LIST

CREMA AL CAFFE'

Coffee Cream

TOTAL TIME: 15
PREP: 10
COOK: 0
LEVEL: easy

INGREDIENTS

MAKES **4** SERVINGS

- 3 YOLKS
- 4 TBSP ICING-SUGAR
- 1 CUP HEAVY CREAM WHIPPED
- 3 TBSP KAHLUA LIQUOR
- 2 TBSP ESPRESSO COFFEE (COLD)
- COOKIES

DIRECTIONS

1. **In** a bowl, beat the egg yolks, adding 4 Tbsp of sugar
2. **Beat** until the mixture has a consistency of mousse (about 3-4 minutes)
3. **Add** the Kahlua and coffee to the egg yolk mixture
4. **Beat** quickly at a reduced speed until creamy
5. **Add** gently the whipped cream
6. **Pour** the cream in a cups and put in refrigerator for 1 hour

READ SHOPPING LIST

From My Florentine Kitchen

SUGGESTIONS

You can use the same recipes (zucchini stuffed) also for stuffed artichokes
In this recipe we served stuffed artichokes with Polenta

Idea for stuffed a mixed vegetables

INGREDIENTS
Zucchini
Tomatoes
Zucchini Flowers

DIRECTION FOR STUFFED TOMATOES
Cut in 2
Scoop out the center flesh with a spoon
Mix 2 Tbsp per tomatoe breadcrumbs
with a mix of basil, cappers, salt and garlic
(minced)
Sprinkle with Extravirgin Oilive Oil
Bake (425 F) for 40 minutes (the tomatoes
need be golden brown)
Serve room temperature

DIRECTION FOR STUFFED ZUCCHINI
FLOWERS
Zucchini Flowers
Eliminate the pistils (gently)
Mixed in a bowl
1 Tbsp of Ricotta per flower
1 Tbsp of Parmigiano per flower
Pepper
Stuff the flower (keeping attention)
Bake for 20 minutes (356 F)
Serve room temperatire

Pasta & Sughi

Pasta Tradizionale

Traditional Pasta

TOTAL TIME: 40
PREP: 20
COOK: 0
LEVEL: easy

INGREDIENTS

MAKES 4 SERVINGS
- I4 OZ. **(400 G)** FLOUR "00"
- 6 EGGS
- I OZ **(30 G)** OLIVE OIL
- I TBSP OF WARM WATER
- I TEASPOON **4 G** SALT

READ SHOPPING LIST

DIRECTIONS

1. **Combine** the eggs (or yolks), salt and other eventual ingredients (as Oil)
2. **Pour** the "liquid" ingredients into your mixer bowl and attach the flat beater
3. **Add** in small stages the flour (mixture if you have the recipe that includes a different quality of flour), turn to speed 2 until it is well mixed
4. **Exchange** flat beater for the dough hook. Turn to speed 2 and knead for about 10 minutes (or how many minutes the recipe needs) , until a dough ball is formed
5. **Remove** dough from bowl and hand-knead for 10 to 15 minutes. NOTE: Good pasta dough should be elastic and pliable, but FIRM (not soft like bread dough). It should not stick to your fingers or fall apart.
6. **Wrap** dough in plastic wrap and put in the refrigerator for a minimum of a half hour (this step is important for the elasticity of the dough)
7. **Remove** dough from refrigerator
8. **Cut** log into slices, then flatten each piece slightly. Spread slices out so they aren't touching and cover with plastic wrap
9. **Using** the widest setting (I on the Kitchenaid), turn mixer to speed 2 and taking one piece of the flattened dough, feed through rollers
10. **Fold** dough in half & roll again
11. **Repeat** a few more times, lightly dusting the sheet of pasta in between each rolling if it feels the slightest bit sticky

CONTINUE TO INCREASE ROLLER SETTING UNTIL DESIRED DOUGH THICKNESS IS REACHED:
3-4 FOR SPAGHETTI
5-6 FOR STANDARD EGG NOODLES, RAVIOLI;
6-7 FOR LASAGNE;
THE THICKNESS DEPENDS ON THE QUALITY OF DOUGH.

1. **Separate** sheets once desired thickness is achieved with a thin towel or piece of plastic wrap dusted with flour, so the dough doesn't dry out too much
2. **Each** sheet can be cut in half or thirds before putting through the cutter to prevent "too long" of strips
3. **After** cutting each sheet, hang to dry on a pasta rack.
4. **Dry** for a minimum of I0 minutes
5. **If** you want to dry the pasta for later use, dry for several hours and then store in airtight plastic bags
6. **When** ready to cook, boil your water (10 liters for Kg. I - 2,6 gallons 2,2 Lb.) and add salt after the water starts boiling (10 gr. for I liter - 0,3 oz for I quart)

ALTERNATIVE
- 1/2 LB. **(250 G)** DURUM WHEAT
- 1/2 LB. **(250 G)** FLOUR "00"
- 4 EGGS
- 2 EGG YOLKS
- I TEASPOON **4 G** SALT

READ SHOPPING LIST

ALTERNATIVE
- **50%** "00" FLOUR
- **50%** DURUM WHEAT SEMOLINA
- **7-10** EGGS PER 2 LB. **(PER I KG)** OF DOUGH

READ SHOPPING LIST

ALTERNATIVE
- **100%** DURUM WHEAT SEMOLINA
- **7-22** EGGS PER 2 LB. **(PER I KG)**
- KNEADING FOR I0 MINUTES AT 33% HUMIDITY

READ SHOPPING LIST

From My Florentine Kitchen

RAVIOLI

Ravioli

TOTAL TIME: 45
PREP: 25
COOK: 0
LEVEL: easy

INGREDIENTS

MAKES 4 SERVINGS

* 14 OZ. **(400 G)** FLOUR "00"
* **6 EGGS**
* 1 OZ **(30 G)** OLIVE OIL
* 1 TBSP OF WARM WATER
* 1 TEASPOON **4 G** SALT

READ SHOPPING LIST

DIRECTIONS

Follow the instructions for making fresh pasta through step 11
thickness (with Kitchenaid 5-6)
Separate sheets once desired thickness is achieved with a thin towel or piece of plastic wrap dusted with flour, so the dough doesn't dry out too much

THE RAVIOLI CAN BE A DIFFERENT SIZE AND SHAPE.
Round - Squared - "half moon" - Triangle - "candy" - Cappelletti
Small - Medium - Large - Huge

We have an unlimited number of ways to make a filling for homemade ravioli.

METHOD ONE (2 SHEETS OF PASTA OVERLAPPING)
MEDIUM SIZE

1. **Lay** one sheet of pasta (long about 19 inch (50 cm))
2. **Take** the ravioli filling out of the refrigerator and place a full Tbsp of it in along of the sheet of a dough (every 4 Inch)
3. **You'll** got about 9 to 10 ravioli per sheet
4. **Cover** the sheet filled with a second sheet
5. **Seal** every single raviolo, helping with the fingers
6. **Every** single raviolo must be well close and without air
7. **Cut** the pasta for separate the ravioli with a specific tools or knife or a pizza cutter
8. **Follow** the size suggested (2 inch - fill - 2 inch)
9. **Try** to give the same shape to every raviolo

METHOD 2 (ONE SHEET OF PASTA FOLDED)
SMALL MEDIUM SIZE

1. **Lay** one sheet of pasta (long about 19 inch (50 cm))
2. **Try** to have a largest sheet of pasta (large like the roller of machine)
3. **Take** the ravioli filling out of the refrigerator and place a small Tbsp of it in along of the sheet of a dough (every 4 Inch)
4. **You'll** got about 9 to 10 ravioli per sheet
5. **Fold** the sheet of pasta and close on self
6. **Seal** every single raviolo with the same cure of the other

From My Florentine Kitchen

FARCITURE PER RAVIOLI: RICOTTA E SPINACI

Filling for Ravioli: Ricotta cheese and spinach

TOTAL TIME: 45
PREP: 25
COOK: 30
LEVEL: easy

INGREDIENTS

MAKES 4 SERVINGS

- 1/2 LB. (250 G.) RICOTTA CHEESE
- 1/2 LB. (250 G.) STEAMED SPINACH
- 2 TBSP EXTRA- VIRGIN OLIVE OIL
- 1/4 LB. (125 G.) GRATED PARMIGIANO
- 1 EGG
- PINCH OF FRESHLY GRATED NUTMEG
- SALT AND PEPPER

READ SHOPPING LIST

DIRECTIONS

1. **Sauté** (medium fire for 5-7 minutes) with 2 Tbsp Extra-virgin olive oil the steamed spinach with a bit of salt and pepper
2. **Wait** until it has gone cold
3. **Chop** the spinach
4. **In a large bowl**, mix ricotta, spinach, Parmigiano, egg and nutmeg
5. **Prepare** the ravioli following the method that you prefer
6. **Bring** a large pot of salted water to a boil
7. **Slide** formed Ravioli into the boiling water. Be careful
8. **Low** the heat (for don't stress the ravioli)
9. **Remove** the ravioli or using a slotted spoon or pour it, gently in stainer

THE BEST SAUCE FOR THIS KIND OF RAVIOLI

BUTTER, SAGE AND PARMIGIANO
Melt the butter
Add the sage
Cook medium/high heat
When the sage is well done (cruncy) add in top of Ravioli
Dreezle with parmigiano

WITH FRESH THYME
Butter, Fresh Thyme and Parmigiano
Melt a butter
Turn off the heat
Add the small leaves of thyme
Toss the ravioli and add grated fresh Parmigiano
BUTTER, TRUFFLE AND PARMIGIANO
Oil Truffle or Butter with truffle or fresh truffle
Melt the butter
Add the truffle
Add in top of Ravioli
Dreezle with parmigiano

Farciture per ravioli: Zucca, Ricotta e Amaretti

Filling for Ravioli: Pumpkin, ricotta cheese and Amaretti cookies

Total Time: 1.15 h
Prep: 30
Cook: 1h
Level: easy

INGREDIENTS

Makes 4 servings

- 1 Pinch NUTMEG
- 1 Potato
- Pepper
- 1/2 Teaspoon SALT
- 1 Egg
- 12.30 oz. (350 g) Pumpkin
- 1/2 Lb. (250 g) Ricotta CHEESES
- 1/2 Cup Parmigiano GRATED
- 1/2 Cup Parmigiano GRATED FOR DREEZLE THE RAVIOLI
- 2 Tbsp OF CUTTER PER PERSON
- 1 Handfull OF Amaretti COOKIES (MINCED)

Read Shopping list

DIRECTIONS

1. Preheat the oven to 356 F (180°)
2. Slice the pumpkin (1 inch thickness)
3. Bake for 25-30 minute (until is soft)
4. At the same time boil the whole potato until is soft (about 20-25 minutes).
5. Wait 10-15 minutes and pass the pumpkin and the potato through potato masher or vegetable mill.
6. Place all ingredients (mashed potato, mashed pumpkin, egg, salt, nutmeg, Parmigiano and ricotta cheese) into a bowl
7. Stir until it obtains a normal pasta texture but softer
8. Prepare the ravioli following the recipe for RAVIOLI

Melt the butter
put in top of ravioli add the fresh grated Parmigiano and the Amaretti cookies

From My Florentine Kitchen

FARCITURE PER RAVIOLI: PATATE E PARMIGIANO (MUGELLO STYLE)

Filling for Ravioli: Potatoes and Parmigiano (Tuscan Style)

TOTAL TIME:	1 h
PREP:	35
COOK:	45
LEVEL:	easy

INGREDIENTS

MAKES 4 SERVINGS

- 4-5 POTATOES
- 1 MEDIUM SIZED ONION - FINELY CHOPPED
- 1 CLOVES OF GARLIC - FINELY CHOPPED
- 4 OZ. PECORINO CHEESE OR PARMIGIANO (GRATED)
- 1 SPRIG OF FRESH ROSEMARY
- 1/4 CUP BUTTER
- 1/4 CUP EXTRA VIRGIN OLIVE OIL
- 2 EGG YOLKS
- NUTMEG
- SALT AND PEPPER

READ SHOPPING LIST

DIRECTIONS

1. **Boil** the potatoes and when they are slightly cooled, puree them
2. **Add** all ingredients: the egg yolks, salt, pepper, nutmeg and cheese
3. **Melt** the oil and butter
4. **Add** the onion and garlic and the rosemary
5. **Let** cool to room temperature, remove the sprig of rosemary, and add to the potato mixture

SAUCE WITH MUSHROOMS

INGREDIENTS

- 5 OUNCES FRESH PORTOBELLO MUSHROOMS
- 5 OZ. PORCINI IF YOU DON'T FOUND FRESH, YOU CAN ALSO USED THE DRY POCRINI (HOW TO PREPARE DRY PORCINI AT PAG.)
- 4 TABLESPOONS GOOD OLIVE OIL
- 1/4 POUND (1 STICK) BUTTER
- 1 SCALLION OR 1 SMALL ONION CHOPPED
- 1 CLOVES OF GARLIC (MINCED)
- 1 TEASPOON MINCED THYME
- 1 CUP GRATED PARMIGIANO

DIRECTIONS

1. **Clean** the mushrooms by wiping them with a dry paper towel. Don't wash them (if you can)! Chop the mushrooms and stems. Slice the caps 1/4-inch thick
2. **Heat** the olive oil and the butter in a large pot.
3. **Add** the chopped scallion or onion and garlic.
4. **Cook** over low heat for a few minutes (5-7), until they begin to golden
5. **Add** the sliced mushroom and cook untill are done while stirring
6. **Add** the fresh thyme
7. **Tossed** the ravioli and add a bit of Parmigiano

GLI GNOCCHI CON LA ZUCCA

Dumplings With Pumpkin

TOTAL TIME: 50
PREP: 15
COOK: 30
LEVEL: easy

INGREDIENTS

MAKES 4 SERVINGS

- 1 PINCH CINNAMON
- 6.30 Oz. (180 G) FLOUR "00"
- 1 PINCH NUTMEG
- 12.30 Oz. (350 G) POTATOES
- PEPPER
- 1/2 TEASPOON SALT
- 1 EGG
- 12.30 Oz. (350 G) PUMPKIN
- 1/2 CUP GRATED PARMIGIANO

DIRECTIONS

1. **Preheat** the oven to 356 F (180°)
2. **Slice** the pumpkin (1 inch thickness)
3. **Bake** for 25-30 minute (until is soft)
4. **A**t the same time boil the whole potatoes until they are soft (about 45 minutes). While still warm, peel and pass through potato masher or vegetable mill.
5. **Wait** 10-15 minutes and pass the pumpkin through potato masher or vegetable mill.
6. **Place** all ingredients (mashed potatoes, mashed pumpkin, egg, flour, salt, nutmeg, cinammon and Parmigiano) into a bowl
7. **Stir** until it obtains a normal pasta texture but softer.
8. **Follow** the same recipe for potato dumplings

READ SHOPPING LIST

From My Florentine Kitchen

GLI GNOCCHI CLASSICI DI PATATE

Traditional dumplings with potatoes

TOTAL TIME: 50
PREP: 15
COOK: 30
LEVEL: easy

INGREDIENTS

MAKES 4 SERVINGS

- 10 OZ. **(300 G)** FLOUR "00"
- **2 LB.** POTATOES
- SALT
- 1 EGG

DIRECTIONS

1. **Wash** the potatoes without peeling them, put them in a pot with salted water and let boil
2. **Still** warm, peel, mash and place on a well floured work surface
3. Add a pinch of salt, flour and knead together until the mixture is firm but soft at the same time
4. **Now** add the egg and continue to knead
5. **Divide** the dough into strands with a thickness of 2.3 cm and start cutting your gnocchi placing them on a floured surface or tray
6. **Finally,** practice characteristics scoring of each dumpling dumplings by sliding the fork and pressing a bit, but not too
7. **Let** stand your gnocchi for 15 minutes, then cook them in a large pot with salted water and drain when they rise to the surface.
8. **Prepare** the sauce that you like and dress your gnocchi

READ SHOPPING LIST

RISOTTO ALLO ZAFFERANO (ALLA MILANESE)

Risotto with saffron (Milanese Style)

TOTAL TIME: 25
PREP: 5
COOK: 20
LEVEL: easy

INGREDIENTS

MAKES 4 SERVINGS

- 3 TBSP PER PERSON CARNAROLI OR ARBORIO OR VIALONE NANO RICE
- 1/2 CUP BUTTER, DIVIDED
- 1 1/2 QUARTS BEEF STOCK
- 3 TBSP BEEF MARROW MINCED (OPTIONAL)
- 1 SCALLION, THINLY SLICED
- 1 TEASPOON SAFFRON POWDER
- SALT TO TASTE
- 1 1/2 CUPS GRATED PARMIGIANO

READ SHOPPING LIST

DIRECTIONS

The choice of rice to make a risotto, is the first important step.

Choose a rice short-grained round or semi-round rice; as Arborio, Vialone Nano, and Carnaroli

1. **Mince** very thinly the scallion (must be like a cream)
2. **Melt** half of the butter in a medium saucepan over low heat
3. **Add** the scallion and beef marrow and cook until the the scallion is soft
4. **Stir** in the rice and sauté it too until it becomes translucent (this will take 5 minutes), stirring constantly
5. **Continue** cooking, stirring and adding broth
6. **After** 10 minutes melt the saffron in a cup of broth and add it to the rice
7. **Continue** cooking as the rice absorbs it, until the rice barely reaches the al dente stage
8. **The** perfect time for total cook 18 minutes
9. **At** this point stir in the remaining butter of butter and the grated cheese, cover the risotto, and turn off the flame
10. **Let** it sit, covered, for two to three minutes, and serve

ADD THE MUSHROOMS... TO MAKE A SUPERB VARIANT!

The classic Risotto with mushrooms is done with Porcini (fresh Porcini) but, if you don't have the fresh you can arrange also with Dry porcini mushrooms.

To prepare dried Porcini steep them in boiling water to cover until they are reconstituted. After draining the Porcini mince, them but keep the steeping liquid. This liquid adds even more concentrated Porcini flavor to the recipe, just make sure you strain it first.

- Follow the istructions at the point 7
- After add the Porcini and the steeping liquid
- Follow again the recipe

From My Florentine Kitchen

CLASSICO RAGÙ DI CARNE QUASI.... ALLA BOLOGNESE
Classic meat sauce (... my personal in Bolognese)

TOTAL TIME:	4 h
PREP:	40
COOK:	3h
LEVEL:	easy

INGREDIENTS

MAKES 4 SERVINGS

- 2 CUPS (250 ML) MEAT BROTH
- 1,7 OZ (50 G.) BUTTER
- 1/2 LB (250 G.) MINCED PORK
- 1 CUP FRESH WHOLE MILK
- 5 TBSP EXTRA VIRGIN OLIVE OIL
- 1,7 OZ (50 G.) TOMATO PASTE
- SALT AND PEPPER
- 2 GARLIC CLOVES, PEELED
- 3 BREAKFAST SAUSAGES*, CASINGS REMOVED
- 1 (17 OUNCE) CAN OF TOMATO PULP
- 1 1/2 CUPS DRY RED WINE
- 2 MEDIUM CARROTS, PEELED AND HALVED
- 1 STALK OF CELERY & THE TOP, HALVED
- 1 MEDIUM YELLOW ONION, PEELED AND QUARTERED
- 1/2 LB (250 G.) GROUND BEEF (NOT TOO LEAN)
- *(I DON'T SUGGEST THE ITALIAN SAUSAGE BECAUSE IN USA IT IS SOLD ONLY WITH FENNEL AND SPICES. THIS QUALITY OF SAUSAGE IS ALMOST UNHEARD OF IN ITALY)

READ SHOPPING LIST

DIRECTIONS

INTRODUCTION

" The Italian Academy of Cuisine "has filed since the 70's, the official recipes of some dishes at the" Chamber of Commerce of Bologna ", among which are also the ragù bolognese
Is certainly important that the cut of beef used in the preparation, "folder" (in Bologna), or the diaphragm of the cow, a very red and juicy meat, low in connective tissue gelatinous but full of flavor, flesh from a short unique characteristics.
Now replaced by lean ground beef
The Pancetta is replaced by the oil (which is, however, more calories!)
It is used tomato instead of tomato paste (the original recipe contains more meat than tomato)
The milk ... nobody uses it!
I propose a my version of Bolognese meat sauce.
These are the traditional ingredients

- FOLDER OF BEEF 300 G
- FRESH BACON 150 G
- YELLOW CARROT 50 G
- CELERY 50 G
- ONION 50 G
- 5 TABLESPOONS TOMATO SAUCE OR EXTRACT TRIPLE 20 G
- WINE RED / WHITE 1/2 CUP
- 200 G OF WHOLE MILK

DIRECTION

1. **Put** the carrots, celery, onion and garlic in a food processor; pulse until finely chopped
2. **Over** a medium flame, heat the olive oil and butter in a large, deep sauce pan with a thick, heavy bottom
3. **To** the pan add the chopped vegetables - until the onions turn clear
4. **Mix** (with hands) the minced pork, the ground beef and the sausages
5. **Continuing** to cook over a medium flame, add the mixture (meats and sausages)
6. **Cook** until it is well done - will become brown and dry -
7. **Add** the wine and simmer until the alcohol evaporates, about 3-5 minutes
8. **Stir** the tomato paste and cook for 2-4 minutes
9. **Add** the tomato pulp and the broth
10. **When** the sauce starts to boil, reduce the heat so that it cooks at the barest simmer, with just an occasional bubble or two.
11. **Cook,** uncovered, for 3 hours, turning down the heat if the sauce starts to scorch. If the sauce dries out before it is done, add a ladle of the the beef broth; and check the seasoning
12. **When** it is ready add salt, pepper and the milk

SUGHI

Il mio Pesto Genovese....

My personal Pesto in Genova style

Total Time: 10
Prep: 10
Cook: 0
Level: easy

INGREDIENTS

Makes 4 servings

1. 2 oz. (55 g) of Fresh Basil
2. 1/2 cup Extravirgin Olive Oil (No strong)
3. 6 Tbsp Grated Parmigiano
4. 2 Tbsp Grated Pecorino
5. 2 Cloves garlic
6. 1 or 2 Tbsp Pine nuts
7. Optional nuts in place with pine nuts
8. Salt (a few grains)

Read Shopping list

DIRECTIONS

1. **In** a blender put garlic and basil and start to mixer 3 to 5 seconds
2. **Add** the pine nuts and mixer again for 3 to 5 seconds
3. **Add** the Cheeses
4. **With** low speed continue to mixer adding the Oil (gradually)

Variant with pistachios!

In place of pine nut add the pistachios!

Consortium of pesto

The original recipe of "Pesto alla Genovese" is a simple and easy but must be with the specified ingredients.

All ingredients are rigorously original from Liguria or from adjacent regions (Toscana, Emilia Romagna).

List of ingredients from Consortium of pesto

1. 2 oz. (55 g) of Basil leaves young and fresh (Basilico Genovese)
2. 1/2 cup Extravirgin Olive Oil (Liguria)
3. 6 Tbsp Grated Parmigiano
4. 2 Tbsp Grated Pecorino (Roman or Tuscan or Sardinian or Sicilian)
5. 2 Cloves garlic
6. 1 or 2 Tbsp Pine nuts
7. Optional nuts in place with pine nuts
8. Salt (a few grains)

Direction

1. **Crush** 1 clove of garlic 30 basil leaves and salt
2. **Add** a little at a time all the basil
3. **Add** the pine nuts
4. **Crush** until you have a creamy
5. **Add** the cheese
6. **Finally** the oil (little by little)

From My Florentine Kitchen

LA MIA SALSA DI POMODORO

My Tomato sauce

TOTAL TIME: 35
PREP: 15
COOK: 30
LEVEL: easy

INGREDIENTS

MAKES 4 SERVINGS

- 2 CARROTS CUT IN CUBE
- 1 ONION MEDIUM CUT IN CUBE
- 1 STICK OF CELERY CUT IN CUBE
- 6 RIPE TOMATOES
- 5-6 LEAVES OF BASIL
- 1-2 CLOVES OF GARLIC
- SALT
- 1 SMALL RED CHILLI
- 5-6 TBSP EXTRAVIRGIN OILVE OIL

READ SHOPPING LIST

DIRECTIONS

1. **Bring** to boil a pot with water and bit of salt and put in the tomatoes
2. **Boil** for 7 to 9 minutes
3. **Drain** the tomatoes, peel
4. **Cut** the tomatoes and remove the seeds
5. **In** a pan pour the Oil with basil and garlic
6. **Add** the carrots, onion and cellery
7. **Cook** until the vegetables are soft
8. **Add** the tomatoes, salt, red chili and cook stirring for 20-25 minutes
9. **With** hand mixer reduce the sauce in a puree
10. **Filter** the puree in a sieve

....and for delicious desserts don't lose our book
TIRAMISU AMORE MIO
30 Easy recipes
for everyone!

Tiramisu Amore Mio

(Tiramisu my love)

30 Easy New Creative Recipes

Authors
Varinia Cappelletti *(Chef Vary)*
and **Edoardo Cecotto**

This is not only a book. It goes beyond!
Through it you'll have access to **photos**,
videos, **updates** and **variations** on recipes.